That Thing

Rich

People Do

[Required Reading for Investors]

Kaye A. Thomas

A Plain Language Guide from

FAIRMARK PRESS INC.

That Thing Rich People Do
Required Reading for Investors

Published by:

Fairmark Press Inc.

www.fairmark.com

First printing of first edition

ISBN-10 0979224888

ISBN-13 9780979224881

Copyright 2010 by Kaye A. Thomas
Printed in the United States of America

Author's Note

Bookstore shelves groan under the weight of countless volumes on investing. Why perpetrate another one?

I started out wanting to *buy* a book on investing, as a gift for the young adults in my family. This would be one of those gifts that reflect the priorities of the giver, of course, not the recipient. No matter, they'll thank me later.

The challenge was finding a book they might actually read. They view this topic as arid terrain where one ventures only when necessary, and then as briefly as possible. One of them, in fact, previewing an earlier version of this preface, took me to task for being so bold as to suggest that readers might find the material interesting. *I doubt that many people are going to be convinced*, she wrote, trying her best to be tactful.

What was needed, I realized, was a book that would lay out the subject as concisely as possible. It would have to be short enough so you might read it in odd moments while warming leftovers or waiting for your computer to reboot, yet it would also have to include the essentials that every investor should know.

Having found no such book I undertook to write one. This is my take on the knowledge you need: required reading for investors, as the subtitle proclaims. For those who are new to the field, it starts at the very beginning. For those who are not, it offers a reality check. Use it to manage your own money or to evaluate the advice you're getting from a professional. But for heaven's sake, *read it*. You'll thank me later.

Kaye Thomas
March 2010

About the Author

Kaye Thomas is best known for his books on tax rules and strategies for investors. He also maintains a popular website at Fairmark.com.

Kaye's professional background is in law rather than finance. His study of investing grew out of the need to integrate investment principles with tax considerations in formulating strategies for capital gains, retirement savings and employee stock options. His law degree is from Harvard Law School, where he served on the *Harvard Law Review.*

Also by the Author

Go Roth!
A complete guide to the Roth IRA, Roth 401k and Roth 403b.

Capital Gains, Minimal Taxes
A complete guide to tax rules and strategies for stocks, mutual funds and exchange-traded options.

Consider Your Options
The leading book on how to handle stock options and other forms of equity compensation received from an employer.

Equity Compensation Strategies
A text for professionals who offer advice on stock options and other forms of equity compensation.

That Thing

People Do

[Required Reading for Investors]

Contents

1

That Thing Rich People Do

I have to do that thing rich people do, where they turn money into more money. Liz Lemon, the character played by Tina Fey in her brilliant comedy series *30 Rock*, makes this vow after she sees the appalling lifestyle she might face if she doesn't shape up financially. In the context of the show, and with the benefit of Tina Fey's delivery, the line is funny and sharp. The idea of investing is so foreign that Liz can't even come up with the word—or perhaps can't bring herself to say it.

Who can blame her? Investing is rarely taught in high school, and few people study it in college. Liz Lemon's wide-eyed innocence on the subject gets a laugh, but most of us finish our education without knowing much more about investing than she does.

So how are we supposed to learn this stuff? From our parents? Employee seminars about the company retirement plan? Osmosis? Liz Lemon asks Jack Donaghy, a corporate executive with an impressive title,* if he can tell her what to do. "With my eyes closed," he replies.

---

* Vice President of East Coast Television and Microwave Programming.

Hey, let me try that:

Frist, start a refular program of sabing . . .

Okay, maybe not with my eyes closed. But the modest goal here is a brief, readable book that starts at the very beginning and provides Liz with the financial literacy needed to make good investment decisions.

We'll stick with approaches that let her money do the work. Liz won't have to become a landlady, and we won't expect her to buy and operate a franchise. She won't have to stay in constant touch with the financial news, or spend long hours poring over the footnotes in a company's financial reports.

On the other hand, we won't be content to tell Liz what to do and how to do it. We'll insist that she learn a bit of the underlying theory. Without that education she's likely to drift into bad habits. She might, for example, conclude her money will be safer if she keeps a lot of it invested in stock of the company where she works. Surveys of investor behavior indicate plenty of people believe this, even after being told otherwise by so-called experts. It takes a little knowledge of how the stock market works to appreciate that the so-called experts know what they're talking about.

Laying a Foundation

2

Turning Money into More Money

Liz may not have realized it, but she got right to the heart of the matter: turning money into more money. That's exactly what the game is all about. Your money can sit there doing nothing, or it can grow into more money. Growing is better. Your money grows when you receive investment income, such as interest or dividends, or when you own something that goes up in value, such as stocks or real estate. The annual rate of growth is called the *return on investment*, or more often just the *return*.

Powerful force

Einstein supposedly said, "Compound interest is the most powerful force in the universe." This would be the genius who invented relativity, not the genius who invented the bagel sandwich.* It's unlikely that either Einstein actually made this remark, but an unwritten law says a book like this has to pretend he did.

---

* Stock in the company that owns Einstein Bros. Bagels trades under the symbol BAGL.

5

It takes just a little arithmetic to see what Einstein was getting at. To make the math easy we'll start with $1,000 and use a 10% interest rate. After a year we have $1,100 because we earned $100 interest. We can take our $100 profit out of the account, but to see the benefit of compounding we have to let it ride for another year.

At the end of the second year we have $1,210. The account grew $110 this time, not just $100, because we started the year with $1,100. We received interest on the original $1,000 plus interest on the first year's interest. Interest on interest: that's what we mean by compound interest.

When you keep your money invested, compounding means the amount of growth gets bigger each year. You earned $100 of interest the first year but $110 the second year, an increase of $10. The third year you would earn $121, an increase of $11 from the second year. Not only does the amount of interest increase each year, but the amount of the *increase* increases each year. And so on. That's what makes compound interest so powerful.

Most people underestimate how much growth they can get from long-term investing. If you ask how long it would take, at 10% interest, to turn $1,000 into $32,000, they're likely to think this is something that won't happen in their lifetime, because the money grows just $100 in the first year. At that rate it would take 10 years to add $1,000, and a hopelessly long 310 years to add $31,000. It's easy to see that compounding will cut the time somewhat, but it still has to take more time than we have on this planet, right?

Actually, it takes about 36 years.

Rule of 72

I didn't need a fancy calculation to figure that out. I used a trick called the *rule of 72*. It tells how long it takes to double your money with compound interest: just divide 72 by the rate of interest. For example, if your investment grows at the rate of 6% per year, divide 72 by 6 to learn it will double in 12 years.

It's a happy coincidence that the magic number is 72 because that number is so easy to divide. It's an even multiple of 2, 3, 4, 6, 8, 9 and 12. Other numbers are easy, too. Is your money growing 7% per year? You can see right away that it will take a little more than 10 years to double.

Getting back to our earlier problem, turning $1,000 into $32,000 involves doubling your money five times:

$$\$1,000 \times 2 \times 2 \times 2 \times 2 \times 2 = \$32,000$$

With your money growing at the rate of 10%, the rule of 72 tells us it would take 7.2 years for each doubling to occur. Five of these doublings would take a total of 36 years.

Ah, to be young

The rule of 72 isn't just a way to figure out how long it takes for your money to double. It helps reveal the significance of getting an early start. At a growth rate of 8%, money you save 9 years before retirement will double once, money saved 18 years before retirement will double twice, and money saved 36 years before retirement can double *four* times. The earlier you start, the less saving will be required to meet your goals.

Many writers have used a version of the following example, where money is assumed to grow at the rate of 8%. One person saves $2,000 per year for just 10 years, from age 20 through 29, and after that simply lets the money grow until age 65. Another person begins saving $2,000 per year at age 30 and continues stashing this amount for 35 years. At age 65, the second person has over $370,000, a darn good result from saving $2,000 per year. But the first person, who started earlier and saved for just 10 years, ends up with more than

$460,000. By starting earlier, that person was able to stop saving at age 30 and still come out ahead.

I don't want to discourage people who are getting a late start. You can begin saving at 40, even 50 or later, and still build a nice nest egg. People who start earlier can build more wealth with a lot less effort, though.

Magnifier effect

The rule of 72 reveals another important fact about investing: over a long period of time, a small difference in the rate of growth can make a huge difference in wealth. We just saw that money can double five times in 36 years if it grows at the rate of 10%. What happens if we use an 8% rate? Divide 8 into 72 and you can see that your money doubles every 9 years. Over that same period of 36 years it will double four times (4 x 9 = 36). Take it down a couple more notches to where you get 6% per year and your money will double just three times in the course of 36 years.

The differences you see in the short run may not seem important. After one year of investing $1,000, you can have $1,060 at 6% or $1,100 at 10%. You'd rather have $1,100 of course, but the difference of $40 is less than some people spend at Starbucks in the course of a week, so it may not seem like a big deal in the *grande* scheme of things. But here are the outcomes after 36 years:

At 6%:	$8,000
At 8%:	$16,000
At 10%:	$32,000

In the long run a 10% rate provides you with *four times as much wealth* as a 6% rate.

Over a lifetime of investing even a small difference in the rate of growth can be significant. An annual hit equal to half of one percent may seem trivial as it occurs, but the cumulative effect after many years of compounding could be tens of thousands of dollars.

The incredible shrinking dollar

Here's another reason your investments need a healthy rate of growth: during all the years you're building up your account, inflation will be gnawing away at its value. We've been through some periods of high inflation and others when it was lower. The average over a long period of time has been around 3% per year.

We can use the rule of 72 to see the effect. Divide 72 by 3 to get 24, the number of years it takes prices to double when inflation runs at 3%. Over a period of 24 years or so you might see the cost of living double, cutting the buying power of your money in half. Anyone above a certain age can bore you to tears talking about how much less they paid for a quart of milk or gallon of gas when they were young.

Your investments need to grow at the rate of inflation just to break even. It's like paddling a boat upstream. To move ahead, you have to propel the boat forward faster than the current carries it back.

To learn how much actual progress you've made we subtract inflation from your rate of growth. The resulting number is called the *real return*. If your investments grow 6% in a year of 2% inflation, your real return is 4%.

Keep this in mind as you plan your long-term investment strategy. A timid approach that produces slow growth may have a real return too small to make much progress, or even to avoid losing ground. Your investments have to be bold enough to produce a real return that can reach your goals.

3

Turning Money into Less Money

Our goal is to make your money grow, so the last thing you want is to lose some of it. Yet risk goes hand in hand with return. Investments that offer greater rewards expose you to more risk. You want safer investments? They're available. Step this way, into the slow growth department.

This tradeoff between risk and reward arises naturally from investors' preferences. Given a choice between two investments that grow at the same rate, they'll buy the safer one, and the riskier one will remain unsold. To attract buyers, a risky investment has to offer richer rewards. As a result, the marketplace for investments always includes safer ones that grow slowly and riskier ones that have the potential for faster growth.

The previous chapter stressed the importance of achieving a faster rate of growth. Pity the poor souls who stopped reading then! Focusing only on higher returns is a recipe for disaster. You need a strategy that offers enough growth without too much risk.

Two kinds of risk

There's more than one kind of investment risk. The first one that comes to mind is the risk that you'll suffer a loss by holding an investment that declines in value. More important is the risk that your investments won't grow enough to meet your goals.

It may seem that these are the same risk, because a loss of value will surely be a setback in growing your wealth. Yet to some extent these risks are opposed to one another. Investments that protect you against loss of value have a slow rate of growth. Rely too heavily on these and you'll hurt your chances of long-term success. To make your money grow fast enough you have to invest in things that fluctuate in value, with some of those zigzags being in the downward direction.

The prediction paradox

It's tantalizing to imagine that we can harness the rapid growth of riskier investments without suffering significant losses. It seems like someone who's really smart about this stuff should be able to figure out when disaster looms and move to safer ground. At the very least, we should be able to notice when a particular stock, or the stock market as a whole, has started to move downward, and step aside until the carnage is over.

That's not how it works. Investment returns have built-in randomness, making it impossible for even the most astute analyst to avoid losses. There's no reliable way to predict when a slide in value will begin or when it will end.

Many people find it hard to accept this notion. The performance of individual stocks, and of the stock market as a whole, is at least partly related to the performance of individual companies and of the economy. Why can't we forecast well enough to avoid steep losses?

There are many reasons we cannot, but the most fundamental one is something I call the prediction paradox, which is a major theme of this book. Here it is in a nutshell. To sell an investment that's about to lose value you need a buyer. No one will pay today's price knowing the investment will be cheaper tomorrow. A reliable prediction is self-defeating. At the same time it tells you to sell, it tells others not to buy.

I hate to say this but I have to: even with the best strategy you're going to suffer losses. Once in a while you'll be blindsided by an event like the stock market disasters of 2000 and 2008. In retrospect it will seem as if you or your advisor should have seen it coming and avoided the worst, but that's an illusion. The prediction paradox guarantees that losses will be unpredictable.

Strategies for uncertainty

There's no way to avoid investment losses, but there are strategies that keep them from derailing your plans. One of the most important is to divide your money among different types of investments: put some in stocks, some in bonds, and perhaps some in real estate, so that losses in one category are softened by better performance in another. Another key is diversification within each category: you need to own many stocks of different types, not just one stock or a few.

Some of the strategies we'll discuss help you buy stocks at lower prices and sell higher without being able to predict performance. Buying at regular intervals will let you take advantage of an effect called dollar cost averaging. Rebalancing your investment account when the division between stocks and bonds gets out of whack will also shift the odds in your favor.

We'll go over all these strategies later, explaining how they help produce good results in the face of uncertainty. Meanwhile keep in mind that over long periods of time, stocks and bonds go up a lot more than they go down. If you participate in the upturns you'll come out ahead despite the occasional setback.

The Investor's Toolbox

4

Taking Stock

This chapter and the next several will introduce stocks, bonds and other investments, and the different types of investment accounts. We'll hold off on building an investment strategy until after you have an idea what's out there.

You: big shot owner

Stocks let you own part of a business. You can buy a slice of Kraft, a dash of Nike or a bit of Intel. Or you can pick Apple, then walk around looking cool and saying "I'm a Mac," until your friends tell you to knock it off.

As a shareholder you'll participate in the company's success, receiving profit payouts called dividends and seeing the value of your shares increase as the company grows. Stocks can turn money into more money faster than other types of investments. In a *bull market*, stocks in general can rise 25% or more in a year, and individual stocks have been known to double in just a few months.

But don't get too excited. The *average* return from stocks over a long period of time is less than seven percentage points above the rate of inflation—and that doesn't take into account taxes and other expenses. There's no sure way to beat that average, and for all we know, the average in future decades may be lower. Worst of all, you can *lose* money in stocks, especially during a *bear market* when overall values are declining. In fact this is one of the few certainties about the stock market: during some periods it will produce losses for even the most astute investors.

Then why bother? One big reason: the average returns for all other categories of investments are lower. If you want growth that will outpace inflation by more than a few percentage points per year, you'll need to invest some of your money in stocks.

Equities. Stocks are sometimes called *equities*. When people talk about equity investments, they aren't talking about fairness and equality. This is just another way of referring to stocks.

Categories of stocks

Something like 7,000 stocks trade on the major exchanges. Investors group them into various categories, and it's useful to know the terminology, especially if you're considering a mutual fund that specializes in one type of stocks.

Size of the company. If we multiply the total number of shares a company has outstanding by the current price of those shares, we get the implicit value of the entire company. This is known as the company's *capitalization*. We shorten that word and refer to giants like Microsoft and General Electric as *large caps*. Companies classified as *small caps* are smaller, of course, but perhaps larger than you might imagine, as they typically have a total value in the hundreds of millions of dollars. We go through periods when big companies prosper and other times when smaller ones produce the most growth, so it makes sense to own both. Avoid speculating on the tiniest pipsqueaks, known as *penny stocks*, though. These are companies too small to trade on the major exchanges. Your broker may offer a way to buy them, but most people who fish in that stream reel in more losses than gains. Say yes to large caps and small caps, no to penny stocks.

Growth versus value. Investors may pay a high price for a stock relative to its current earnings if they expect profits to rise rapidly. In that case it would be considered a *growth stock*. When investors are less optimistic about growth, they'll pay a lower price relative to current earnings. These are called *value stocks* because you're buying a greater amount of current earning power for each dollar you spend. Some mutual funds specialize in one type or the other. Neither one is inherently better: we go through periods when growth stocks surge ahead, only to fall behind when value starts to shine.

Sectors. Stocks can be divided according to the sector of the economy in which the company operates, such as energy, consumer products, or health care. Technology stocks seem to get more attention than all the others combined. Despite their allure (or perhaps partly because of it) these stocks perform no better than others that are less glamorous, so smart investors diversify across all the major sectors of the economy.

Geography. You can buy mutual funds that invest only in the United States, but there are others that invest in specific areas of the world and some that invest throughout the world. You may feel more comfortable sticking with U.S. stocks, but there's an advantage in looking overseas for part of your portfolio: foreign stocks sometimes do well when U.S. stocks perform poorly, helping to smooth out your investment results.

Investing in stocks

One way to invest in stocks is in a brokerage account. This is much like a bank account, and you open it the same way, filling out forms and depositing a check. Then you can issue instructions for the purchase or sale of shares using the appropriate symbol. An order to "buy 100 MSFT" would make you an owner of Microsoft, just like Bill Gates, except he might own a few more shares than you.

Many people take satisfaction in this form of investing. They may enjoy selecting stocks for their portfolio, or simply like the idea of having a direct ownership interest in companies they admire. You can invest in stocks without managing a brokerage account, though. Mutual funds, discussed later, are more convenient and less expensive.

5

Taking Interest

Governments and large businesses often have to borrow large sums of money, more than they can get from any one source. They break the loan up into smaller pieces so many investors can get in on the act. These investments can go by various names, such as *notes* or *debentures*. We'll use the term *bonds* to include all these items, except for the "cash" investments described in the next chapter.

What is a bond?

Suppose your friend needs a loan. He says he'll give you a piece of paper saying how much he'll pay and when, with how much interest. You can keep that paper and receive all the payments until the loan is fully repaid—but your friend says you're allowed to sell it to someone else (assuming you can find a buyer), and if you do that, all the future payments will go to the person who bought it from you.

A bond is like that piece of paper. It represents the right to receive a specified series of payments. The *issuer* of the bond is the company or government that borrowed the money. The *holder* of the bond is the person who has the right to receive payments. It could be someone who loaned money to the issuer, but more often it's a subsequent purchaser of the bond.

If you take out a car loan or a mortgage, each monthly payment includes the amount of interest you owe for that month plus a partial repayment of the loan. Bonds generally don't work that way. Typically they pay interest every six months, and repay the entire loan in a single payment at the end. The date when this final payment comes due is called the *maturity date.*

Bonds are the main alternative to stocks for long-term investing. On average they don't grow your account as fast as stocks, so it usually doesn't make sense to put all your money in bonds. You get a good tradeoff when you put *some* of your money in bonds, though, because this approach can limit the damage from a severe downturn in the stock market without slowing your average rate of growth too much.

Gentlemen prefer bonds. Bond investments are more sedate than stocks. Imagine an English butler serving tea. He may on occasion raise or lower his eyebrows, but only a millimeter or two. "Thank you, Jeeves." "Not at all, sir."

Lower risk is to be expected. The issuer of a bond has a legal obligation to make the payments. A company may pay dividends on its stock, but it isn't required to do so. In fact, a company isn't allowed to pay dividends if it lacks the money to make payments on its bonds. When things turn ugly, shareholders suffer before bondholders, and usually suffer more.

Yet bonds are not risk-free, and you can lose money even if the issuer makes all the payments. To see why, imagine that you've paid $1,000 for a ten-year bond calling for interest payments at the rate of 5%. For the next decade you expect to receive $50 per year in interest payments, and at the end of that time you'll also receive repayment of the $1,000.

Shortly after you buy this bond interest rates go up, so that companies issuing bonds similar to this one now have to pay 8%. An investor with $1,000 to spend on a newly issued bond can receive $80 per year in interest payments, so he certainly wouldn't pay $1,000 for *your* bond, which is still paying just $50 per year. If you try to sell your bond you'll find the value has gone down.

You may avoid an actual loss if you continue holding the bond until the final payment. But then you've spent years receiving payments of $50 per year when other investors were raking in $80 per year. What's more, chances are that your investment has suffered more erosion from inflation than you expected when you bought the bond, because an increase in interest rates is often due to a rise in inflation.

So bonds don't offer a free lunch. They're less risky than stocks, but when interest rates go up you can lose money even if you bought the safest bonds available.

Remember, an increase in interest rates may be good for someone who's *about to* buy bonds, but it's bad for anyone who *already owns* them. And of course the reverse is true when interest rates go down.

Categories of bonds

Like stocks, bonds come in a variety of flavors. Some are more suitable for ordinary investors, and some have special tax treatment.

Making the grade. To make it easier for investors to decide which bonds to buy and how much to pay for them, bond issuers obtain ratings from companies that specialize in evaluating the level of certainty that payments will be made as promised. Bonds with high enough ratings are called *investment grade* bonds. These bonds are not 100% certain to be repaid, but defaults are relatively rare.

Bonds that fall below this standard carry a higher rate of interest to compensate for the greater risk. People trying to sell low-rated bonds stress this positive feature, calling them *high-yield bonds*. Nearly everyone else calls them *junk bonds*. "High-yield" sounds desirable and "junk" is unappealing, but these terms mean the same thing when we're talking about bonds.

Junk bonds aren't necessarily a bad investment, but it's difficult to judge whether the higher payoff is enough to justify the greater risk. The conventional wisdom is that ordinary investors should allocate at most a small portion of their portfolio to junk bonds.

State and local bonds. State and local governments don't issue stock but they often have to borrow money by issuing bonds. Holders of these bonds (often called *municipal bonds* or *munis* for short) are allowed to exclude the interest from income when they file their federal income tax returns. Better still, states that impose an income tax generally provide an exemption for interest on bonds issued by that state and its political subdivisions.

The prospect of receiving interest without paying income tax creates so much demand for these bonds that state and local governments are able to issue them at relatively low rates of interest. For example, when regular bonds are paying 5.0%, a tax-exempt bond might pay 3.5%. Even at this lower rate, the tax-exempt bond would be attractive to someone in the 40% tax bracket. After paying 40% tax on the 5% interest from a regular bond she's left with only 3.0%, so the tax-exempt bond at 3.5% works out better. You wouldn't choose the tax-exempt bond if you were in the 20% bracket, though. You could pay tax on the 5% interest from the regular bond and still be left with 4.0%, which is better than you get from the tax-exempt bond.

So these bonds are suitable only for investors in high tax brackets. Others should avoid them because the tax benefit isn't great enough to make up for the lower rate of interest. Also, you should never hold these bonds in an IRA or other retirement account, or in a 529 or Coverdell education savings account, because you would get a lower rate of interest without any offsetting tax benefit.

Treasury obligations. In their infinite wisdom, our elected representatives make it impossible for the United States government to pay its bills without borrowing, so the Treasury issues debt obligations in incomprehensible amounts. These bonds pay interest that is exempt from state and local income tax but taxable on your federal Form 1040. The benefit of avoiding state and local income tax is significant to some investors, but isn't a big enough factor in the overall bond market to affect interest rates very much. These bonds pay almost as much interest as the safest corporate bonds, so it's okay to hold them in a retirement account.

Some of the bonds offered by the U.S. Treasury provide inflation protection. Interest for a given period is a base amount increased by the amount of inflation during that interval. These bonds hold their value better than others if the inflation rate goes up, but may perform poorly when prices are stable.

Investing in bonds

Some stockbrokers make it possible to buy and sell individual bonds in your brokerage account. You can buy U.S. government obligations directly from the Treasury on the Internet, at TreasuryDirect.gov. For most investors, it's easier to invest in a bond mutual fund. Just make sure you find one where the costs of investing are low.

Andrew Tobias, one of my favorite authors in this field, doesn't much like the idea of using a bond fund when you can eliminate the middleman by buying Treasury obligations directly from the government. You can learn more about bonds from his book, *The Only Investment Guide You'll Ever Need.* He grudgingly admits you might choose a low-cost bond fund for its convenience, though, and that's what I've done. Personally, I'd have to see more of an advantage in managing my own bond investments before I took on the task.

6

Playing Safe

Our third category of investments is *cash*. This term has a special meaning in the world of investing. We aren't talking about actual currency you carry around in your wallet. These are investments that offer a way to earn interest with little or no risk of loss.

By now I'm sure you can guess what I'll say next. An investment that offers this much security is necessarily going to inch forward at snail speed. In fact, you should consider yourself lucky if your cash investments grow at all, after taking inflation into account.

These investments have their uses, though. They provide a good way to start accumulating savings when you haven't built up enough to make other investments. After that, they provide a place for any money you want to keep as an emergency stash, so you don't have to cash in other investments when your car needs a repair, for example. They also offer something productive to do with money you'll need in the near future. Is there a tuition payment due in the fall? Are you going to owe taxes next April? Money you've set aside to meet these obligations shouldn't be in stocks or other investments that can lose value, but you may as well earn at least a little interest until the payment is due.

Cash can also act as a damper on risk in a portfolio of stocks and bonds, particularly as you approach the time you expect to begin using the money. In the years leading up to retirement, or after you're retired, you may be concerned that a period in which stocks and bonds *both* perform poorly could deal a serious blow to your plans. Adding cash to the mix may provide the level of security you're seeking.

Investing in cash

Here are some of the ways you can earn interest without taking the kind of risk associated with bonds.

Savings accounts. Most banks offer savings accounts and make it easy to open one. (I use the term *bank* broadly to include savings and loans, credit unions and similar institutions.) The minimum starting balance is usually small, and many banks charge no fees for establishing and maintaining these accounts. At the end of each month the bank adds money to the account in the form of interest.

There's a lot to be said for this way of building wealth. It's simple, low-cost and convenient. It's also entirely risk-free, up to a limit,* if you save at a bank where deposits are guaranteed by the United States government (look for a sign that says *FDIC insured*).

Money markets. Money market accounts, and money market funds, serve essentially the same purpose as savings accounts, offering a way to earn interest without having your money tied up or taking much risk. Not all of these offerings

---

* The basic limit was boosted to $250,000 in the financial crisis that began in 2008, but at this writing is scheduled to drop to the previous level of $100,000 at the end of 2013. Visit fdic.gov for details.

are FDIC insured, and those that are not offer somewhat
higher returns because of the basic tradeoff that has now
become familiar: investors generally won't take more risk
unless they get higher returns. Yet we're talking about a tiny
increase in risk, so you shouldn't expect much of a boost in
earnings when you choose an uninsured money market fund.

Certificates of deposit. *Certificates of deposit* (or *CDs*) are
similar to bonds. You're lending money to a bank or other
financial institution in return for interest payments, but you
can choose a short time period if you prefer, and here again
FDIC insurance may be available. Unless you're sure you can
wait out the entire term, check to see what would happen if
you cash in early. There's usually a penalty of some sort, but
it may be nothing more than losing a portion of the interest
you've earned.

Stable value funds. Generally these funds are available
only in employer plans such as 401k or 403b plans. They
strive to offer higher returns than you can get from a money
market fund with less risk exposure than a conventional bond
fund. It's too soon to know how these relatively new funds
will perform over the long term, but it seems reasonable to
expect both risk and return to fall somewhere between the
levels for money market funds and bond funds.

7

Getting Real

I've made a promise not to compete with the authors whose books explain difficult, time-consuming investments. I may be leaving money on the table, but a deal's a deal. We're going to stick with easy ways to invest.

Owning and managing rental real estate doesn't qualify. Things can run smoothly, but more often they don't. Plumbing emergencies in the middle of the night. Noise complaints. Pet problems. Failure to pay rent. Being a landlord means investing time as well as money.

Investment real estate has other disadvantages relative to stocks and bonds. Expenses of buying, owning and selling are all higher. It's hard to diversify as a landlord: even if you own multiple properties they're likely to be in a single geographic area where a sour local economy can affect values. You can usually sell stocks and bonds instantly, but it may take months to find a buyer for real property.

What about growth? Real estate values sometimes rise sharply, but the *average* rate of growth is unimpressive. In the second edition of his book *Irrational Exuberance*, Robert Shiller gave the results of a study finding that over a period of more than 100 years, home prices rose less than half a percentage point per year faster than the rate of inflation. As a pure investment play, real estate is about as bad as it gets.

Rental properties can be rewarding despite these drawbacks. When things are working right, lease income exceeds mortgage interest and other expenses, producing positive cash flow and setting the stage for a profitable sale of the property. People have been known to build substantial wealth as landlords. In my book, though (and after all, this *is* my book), direct participation in rental real estate should be considered a business rather than an investment.

Another way to invest in real estate is to own your own home, a purchase that can offer unique advantages. You enjoy tax benefits that aren't available for other investments, provide shelter for yourself and loved ones without paying rent, and take a special pride in your home and community. Homeownership isn't for everyone, but it makes great sense for many of us, provided we resist any pressure we may feel to buy a home we can't afford.

Investing in real estate

There's a way to invest in real estate without all the difficulties described earlier, and a reason you may want to do so. A *real estate investment trust*, or *REIT* (rhymes with "treat"), is a company that invests in real property. They issue shares you can buy and sell like shares of stock, using the money to buy real estate and hire people to manage it.

Like any other type of business, REITs go through good times and bad. The thing that makes them attractive, apart from an average rate of return that compares reasonably well with other investments, is that their good times can occur during bad times for other investments, and vice versa. You may gain a smoother ride by putting part of your portfolio into a REIT, or a mutual fund that holds REIT shares. Remember, though, if you own a home you already have a sizeable investment in real estate and may not need more.

8

Our Mutual Friends

A mutual fund isn't really a different kind of investment. It's a way to invest in the ones we've already discussed. These funds pool together money from many investors and use it to buy stocks, bonds or other investments. A single purchase can make you the indirect owner of a diversified portfolio.

At last count there are over 8,000 mutual funds in the United States. That's more than the number of Taco Bells, which is pretty amazing, especially if you've ever tried the Burrito Supreme®. Some of these funds invest in both stocks and bonds. Others stick with one or the other. Among the stock funds, some buy all kinds of stocks while others focus on a particular category, such as health care companies, or small cap value stocks. Bond funds specialize as well. You can find one that focuses on municipal bonds issued in the state of California, for example.

We haven't talked about strategy yet, but when we do you'll see that mutual funds make it easier to put a good one in place. They can help you diversify, keep investment costs under control, and maintain a proper balance between stocks and bonds. This is why they form the core holdings, and often the only holdings, of so many investors.

Buying and selling

When you buy shares your money goes into the fund, where the managers use it to make investments. Your results aren't based on the particular purchases made with your money, though. All investors in the fund share *mutually* in the results of all its investments.

The price you pay for each share in the fund is determined by adding up the total value of all the fund's assets, subtracting any liabilities (money the fund owes), and dividing by the total number of shares held by all investors. The managers calculate this number at the end of each day the stock market is open. If you place an order to buy or sell before the market opens, or while it's open, you'll get the price as of the end of that day. An order placed after the market closes, or on a day when there is no trading, is priced at the end of the next day the market is open. Share prices can be found in many newspapers and on the Internet, sometimes labeled *NAV*, which stands for *net asset value*. The same price is used to determine how much money you receive when selling shares.

When buying mutual fund shares you don't say how many shares you want. Instead, you say how many dollars you want to invest. The fund company divides your investment by the share price to find the number of shares you get, down to three decimal places. You might add $500 to your account, for example, and become the proud owner of 20.686 shares.

Money market funds work a little differently. These low-risk, slow-growth funds try to keep their share value equal to a dollar per share. As your money grows you receive more shares, so the number of shares you own stays the same as the dollar value of your investment. The only exception would be when a money market fund suffers a loss big enough to drive its share price below a dollar, an extremely rare occurrence.

Mutual fund dividends

At least once a year, and sometimes more often, a mutual fund pays out dividends to its shareholders. Most people choose to have dividends automatically reinvested in the same mutual fund, and in this case you may not even notice anything happened.

Actually, two things happen at the same time. Keep in mind that the value of a share comes from the value of the fund's assets, including cash. That means the dividend payment reduces the value of each share—for example, if shares were worth $22.85 immediately before a dividend of $1.45, they'll be worth $21.40 immediately after. At the same time, the dividend is reinvested, so you own more shares. These two effects cancel each other out and your wealth remains unchanged. A sudden drop in the share price doesn't necessarily mean you lost money; it may simply mean the fund paid a dividend.

Investing in mutual funds

If you're choosing investments for your 401k or similar account where you work, you select your mutual funds in the manner indicated by the humans in the human resources department. For an investment account you set up on your own, you have two basic approaches.

The traditional way to buy mutual fund shares is to establish an account with the fund company sponsoring the funds you want to buy. The larger companies offer dozens of funds including a variety of stock funds, several types of bond funds, and others that combine stocks and bonds into a single fund. You can invest in a single fund or divide your money among different types of funds according to the strategy you've chosen to pursue. If you later decide to adjust your portfolio it's easy to move money from one fund to another. Using this approach, if you want to invest in funds offered by more than one company, you would establish an account at each of those companies.

Having more than one account can be an advantage as you gain access to the guidance and other resources each company offers its customers. On the other hand, consolidating at one company can reduce paperwork and perhaps avoid confusion. Many companies—both mutual fund companies and brokerage firms—offer accounts that allow you to buy shares in funds of more than one mutual fund company. An account at Fidelity, for example, will allow you to invest in Fidelity's own funds and also in funds of many of Fidelity's competitors.

These accounts offering one-stop shopping don't provide access to shares of *all* mutual fund companies, however. The list of funds available at one firm won't be the same as at another. Note also that when you use an account at one firm to invest in shares offered by a different one, you may incur transaction fees or other expenses that wouldn't apply if you invested directly by setting up an account with the company that offers the mutual fund.

In later chapters we'll see that there's no way to know which mutual funds will perform best and no advantage in hopping frequently from one to another. You can achieve excellent results while investing in the funds of a single company. If you decide you want to hold funds from more than one company, you'll either have to set up accounts with each one or find a brokerage or mutual fund firm that provides access to the funds you want to buy.

SRI Funds

There's a special category of mutual funds called *SRI funds*, where SRI stands for *socially responsible investing* or *sustainable and responsible investing*. These funds won't invest in a company that doesn't meet standards set by the fund. Often they automatically exclude certain types of businesses (alcohol, tobacco and firearms, for example) and screen for other issues such as product safety, environmentalism, workplace conditions and community relations. Some people argue that you give up growth opportunities when you restrict your investments to socially responsible companies. Others suggest that in the long run these companies are likely to excel, producing good investment results along with social benefits.

Exchange-traded funds

The end-of-day pricing method described earlier for regular mutual funds doesn't apply to *exchange-traded funds*. As the name suggests, investors buy and sell *ETF* shares on an exchange, the same way they buy and sell shares of stock. You don't have to wait until the end of the day to know the share price: if the stock market is open, you get the price that's available at the time you place the order.

The opportunity to trade shares during the day doesn't provide any benefit to ordinary investors. ETFs do offer a definite advantage, however—to brokerage firms that get to charge a commission every time you buy or sell shares. The costs you incur in buying and selling shares can leave you with worse performance than if you invested in a regular mutual fund that holds the same stocks. What's more, although ETFs are designed to make their shares trade at a price that's close to the value of the fund's assets, it won't always be exactly on target, so you can pay more than the assets are worth when buying or get less than they're worth when selling.

Hedge funds ~ *Gen., Avoid*

It's unlikely you'll ever want to invest in a hedge fund, but you may hear about them and wonder what's going on. They're similar to mutual funds but operate with fewer restrictions. As a result, they're considered suitable only for "sophisticated" investors—people with so much money they can afford to take unusual risks. You need to be wealthy before they'll accept you as an investor.

Don't feel left out, though. While hedge funds sometimes succeed brilliantly, they're subject to the same law that governs all of investing: for faster growth, you must take greater risk. Plenty of people have lost, and lost big, on these investments. Furthermore, the fee structure is highly disadvantageous to investors. Compensation to the managers may include 20% or more of the profit in a good year while investors bear 100% of the loss in a bad one. The opportunity to invest in a hedge fund is a dubious privilege.

9

You Bet Your Life

How long will you live? Not sure? Then you may need life insurance (in case you die too soon) or an annuity (in case you live too long). Here's a quick look at how they fit into the world of investing.

Life insurance

The main purpose of life insurance is to reduce the financial hardship your survivors would suffer if you died. The untimely death of a breadwinner can leave loved ones without the support they expected, derailing plans and perhaps leading to a lower standard of living. The loss of a homemaker can be just as costly, requiring a surviving spouse or partner to pay for services or reduce the time spent earning a living.

The simplest and least costly form of life insurance is *term* insurance, which covers you for a specified period of time. It's often provided as an employment benefit and younger folks can get it at a modest cost, barring a serious health problem. It becomes less affordable as you move toward and into retirement years, but you may have no need for it then, as your loved ones are no longer counting on you to produce an income.

At some point you'll surely hear a sales pitch for some form of permanent life insurance. Depending on the design, it may be called *whole life*, *universal life*, or *variable universal life* (*VUL*). These policies have an investment component, which may allow the policy to build up a cash value that enhances the death benefit or provides a convenient source of borrowing. The presentation will dwell on these and other attractive features, and may include projections showing how the policy will make you or your beneficiaries wealthy.

These policies do indeed produce a great deal of wealth— but often for the people who sell them, not the people who buy them. Sales commissions and other expenses built into the policies can be a huge drag on investment performance. As a rule you will do far better if you buy term insurance and put the additional dollars you would have spent on permanent insurance into a sensible, low cost mutual fund. Whole life policies can make sense for some people, such as multi-millionaires who use them to fund estate taxes. Most people should stick with term life, and get a competitive quote before buying.

Annuities

Annuities are contracts with insurance companies that promise to make a stream of payments, usually for the lifetime of the owner of the policy, or the joint lives of that person and his or her spouse. Their main purpose is the opposite of life insurance. Instead of providing money to replace lost income if you die earlier than expected, an annuity prevents you from running out of money if you live longer than expected.

The simplest form of annuity is called an *immediate fixed annuity*. The amount of the monthly payout is determined at the time you buy the annuity (which is why it's *fixed*), and payments begin right after you buy it (which is why it's *immediate*). People often buy this type of annuity around the time they retire, using a portion of their retirement savings. There's no need to buy ahead of time: unlike life insurance, an annuity won't become less affordable (or less available) as you grow older.

Most experts agree that an immediate fixed annuity can make sense for many people. Another type, called a *variable annuity*, is more controversial. You can buy this type of policy many years before you need the payments. In the meantime, a portion of the money you pay to the insurance company goes into *subaccounts* that resemble mutual funds. The payout you eventually receive depends in part on the performance of these subaccounts (which is why this is called a *variable* annuity). Many of these annuities have features designed to make them seem attractive. For example, you may have a form of protection against losses even if part of your money is in a subaccount that invests in stocks.

The main problem is that many of these offerings arc laden with expenses so high as to virtually guarantee inferior investment performance. During the life of the policy this added drain, above and beyond what you would experience in comparable mutual fund investments, can be two percentage points per year or more. Recall that this is a big enough differential to cut your wealth in half over a long enough period of time.

This added expense would be bad enough if you were free to change your mind and switch to a better investment after buying the annuity. Yet these policies often require surrender charges for a period of years after purchase. Expenses will gnaw away at your money if you leave it in the policy, but surrender charges may take an even bigger bite if you pull it out.

Variable annuities are not universally bad. Many teachers, medical professionals and others working for nonprofit organizations participate in retirement plans that offer TIAA-CREF annuities, which are highly regarded. In a later chapter we'll learn that the investment expenses of mutual funds vary widely, and you can buy low-cost variable annuities through some of the same companies that offer low-cost mutual funds. A fee-only advisor can help you select one if you feel this type of investment is right for you.

These are not the variable annuities that are most strenuously promoted, however. If you see a glossy sales pitch for variable annuities, it's more likely to come from someone who earns a generous commission for persuading clients to make this investment. If you're tempted, take some time to weigh the alternatives. Bear in mind that all the attractive features that are built into the annuity come at a price, and often the price is higher than it should be. These are complicated contracts with hidden costs and no easy escape. And remember, annuities get cheaper, not more expensive, as you grow older. You can wait and get a simpler, less expensive, immediate fixed annuity when the need arises.

10

Account for Yourself

The investments we're talking about here require you to have an account of some kind. You may want to have more than one, because some are designed for specific purposes. Here's a summary of what's out there.

Plain vanilla

Anyone over the age of 18 can open a regular investment account. You'll need to fill out some forms and deposit a check. Many companies impose a minimum starting balance, which can be as low as a few hundred dollars but is often set at a few thousand dollars, and can be higher. Sometimes you can start with a smaller amount if you set up automatic monthly additions to the account.

Within the account you can make any investments that are available for that type of account at the company where you established it. Generally you can switch from one investment to another whenever you want, although you may encounter restrictions for some items. You can add to your account or withdraw money whenever you want.

You have to pay income tax on any interest or dividends earned in this account, even if you don't touch the money and have it reinvested. Sales of items such as stocks or mutual fund shares also have to be reported on your tax return. A profit on the sale is called a *capital gain* and may be taxed at a lower rate if you held the investment more than a year. A *capital loss* can reduce your income tax, subject to limitations.

Most other types of accounts offer a way to postpone paying tax on your investment earnings, or avoid paying tax altogether. They come with restrictions, though, limiting the amount you can contribute and potentially hitting you with a penalty if you use the money too soon or for the wrong purpose. The tax benefits are powerful enough to make these accounts worthwhile when they fit with your goals, but a regular account, sometimes called a *taxable account*, offers a place to stash your other money.

Saving where you work

Many employers offer a way to have part of your paycheck go into a retirement account. The most common plan is called a *401k* (for a section of the tax law). Some employers have *403b* plans, which work pretty much the same way.

You may have to fill out a form to get started, although many employers sign you up automatically, putting part of your paycheck into an account. From time to time you're allowed to change the amount you pay into the plan or change the way the money is invested.

Generally you pay no income tax on the portion of your pay that goes into the retirement account. You also pay no tax on investment earnings while they remain in the account. You have to pay tax on all that money, though (your original contributions and the investment earnings) when you take the money out, unless you're moving it to another retirement account (a *rollover*). Also, with some exceptions, you'll be hit with a 10% penalty, in addition to regular income tax, if you use money from this account before age 59½. Roth accounts work differently, but we'll talk about them later.

The benefit of being able to delay paying tax on your contributions and the investment earnings helps your money grow faster, and can make a big difference over a long period of time. You come out ahead, even though you eventually have to pay tax when you're ready to use the money.

Some employers make matching contributions when you add to your account. They might add $25 for every $100 you put in, for example. That's like getting a three- or four-year head start on making your money grow, a really sweet deal.

Most of these plans offer a limited menu of investment choices. That's okay if the options are good, as is usually the case. A few good choices are better than a lot of poor ones.

The money you contribute to this account is fully *vested*, which means you get to keep it even if you get fired for that stunt you pulled in the photocopy room. Matching contributions may not be vested until you've worked there for a period of time, so it's possible to forfeit some or all of that money on termination of employment.

Although your contributions are vested, you can't simply take that money back whenever you want. You may be able to borrow against the account or take a hardship distribution, but the satisfaction of closing your fist around a check for the full balance normally arrives only after you stop working for that employer.

Overall these plans are a good deal except when you get matching contributions, and then they're a great deal. If you don't have one available, you can duplicate many of the benefits in a retirement account you set up on your own, which brings us to . . .

Traditional IRAs

Individual retirement accounts, or IRAs, have been around since the 1970s. They provide a way to set up your own retirement account instead of, or in addition to, any retirement savings you have where you work. Since 1998 we've had a choice between the Roth IRA, discussed later, and the original type, called the *traditional IRA*.

You can set up an IRA at a bank, mutual fund company, brokerage firm or other financial institution. As long as you're under age 70½, you can add to a traditional IRA any year you have income earned by working (as opposed to other types, such as pension income or investment income). If you're married you can rely on your spouse's earned income, and if you're divorced, alimony counts as earned income (though child support does not).

In broad outline traditional IRAs work the same way as a 401k account. Normally you get a deduction for the amount you add to the account. (If you participate in a 401k or similar plan and your income is above limits set in the tax law you may lose this deduction, though you can still make nondeductible contributions.) You pay no tax on investment earnings as they build up in the account, so the money can grow faster than it would in a regular investment account. You pay tax when you take money out of the account, except when rolling it over to another retirement account. Subject to exceptions, you also pay a 10% penalty if you take the money out before age 59½.

But there are important differences between IRAs and 401k accounts. The dollar limit for IRA contributions is smaller. You won't get matching contributions from your employer. You can't borrow from your IRA. You *can* take money out whenever you want (assuming you haven't tied it up in an investment you can't convert to cash), although the tax cost of using IRA money before age 59½ can be punishing. Your investment choices are limited only by the offerings of the firm where you set up your IRA, and if you find those options inadequate you can move your IRA to another firm.

A traditional IRA can be an excellent choice, though it's usually better to save where you work if you get matching contributions. Before making this choice, consider whether you would be better off with a Roth IRA.

Roth accounts

Named for a senator who pushed for their creation, *Roth IRAs* offer another choice for your retirement savings. High-income individuals can't contribute to Roth IRAs, but otherwise the main requirement is to have earned income as described above for traditional IRAs. You can add to a Roth even if you participate in a 401k where you work.

You don't get a tax deduction when you add to a Roth, but if you follow all the rules you'll be able to take money out of the account, including earnings that have built up over the years, entirely tax-free. Traditional IRAs allow you to *postpone* paying tax, but a Roth lets you build wealth that's permanently tax-free. To get the full benefit you need to have a Roth for at least five years and wait until you're at least 59½ before you withdraw the investment earnings.

Many employers also offer Roth accounts in their 401k or 403b plan. The overall tax treatment is the same: no deduction when money goes in, but tax-free distributions when you meet the dual age requirements: five years for the account and 59½ for yourself. You can select these accounts even if your income is too high to contribute to a Roth IRA.

I like Roth accounts—in fact, I've written a book about them, called *Go Roth!* In a Roth you can build just as much wealth as in a traditional IRA or 401k, but you end up with more *spendable* wealth because distributions aren't taxed.

Also, if you're ever forced to take money from the account in an emergency, before age 59½, the tax hit is much less punishing because it applies only to the investment earnings, not the money you contributed.

Traditional accounts can be better, though, especially for people who are closing in on retirement (say, within the next 10 or 15 years) and expect to be in a lower tax bracket after they stop working. You should also strongly consider a traditional account if that's the only kind offered at work and you can get matching contributions from your employer, because you won't get a match in a Roth IRA you set up on your own.

College savings accounts

People save for other goals besides retirement, and college is a big one. We have two special types of accounts for this purpose. In keeping with customary practice, one is named for a section of the tax law and the other for a now-deceased senator. Both types offer a Roth-like benefit: you don't get a deduction when you put money in the account, but the account isn't taxed while it's growing, and you can withdraw investment earnings tax-free if they're used for qualifying education expenses.

The ones known as *529 accounts* are mostly sponsored by individual states. You don't have to use them to attend state schools though, or even schools located in the state. In fact, you don't have to live in a state to use its plan. You may find that you can claim a benefit of some kind on your state income tax return when using your own state's plan, but otherwise you're free to shop around for the one you like best.

You can contribute as much as you want to a 529 account, up to the full cost of a college education, although you may have to deal with gift tax issues if you pump in very large amounts in a single year. The main issue with these accounts is a limited menu of investment choices, together with restrictions on how often you can move money from one option to another. But some states offer high-quality choices, and it isn't a good idea to make frequent changes in your investments anyway.

Coverdell accounts resemble IRAs more closely—in fact, they were originally called education IRAs. They have a modest annual contribution limit ($2,000 at this writing) and you aren't allowed to contribute if your income is too high. You can set them up just about anywhere, though, and your investment choices are as flexible as for IRAs, permitting you to make changes whenever you wish.

Custodial accounts for minors

A person under the age of 18 can own an investment account only if it is set up as an *UTMA* account under the Uniform Transfers to Minors Act. An adult known as the custodian (often but not always a parent) has to sign the relevant forms and make decisions about how to invest the money and when and how it can be spent. Control of the account passes over to the minor at age 18 or 21, depending on state law and choices made at the time the account was established.

Money in these accounts can be the minor's own earnings (perhaps from a summer job) or gifts from parents or other relatives. Either way, the minor is the *owner* of the account, even while an adult remains in control. That means the account's investment income goes on the child's income tax return. It also means the custodian isn't allowed to take this money away or use it except for the benefit of the child. When control passes, the child can use the account as he or she wishes—which may not be as the parent or other relative envisioned when setting up the account.

For these and other reasons, custodial accounts are not a good choice for sizeable transfers of wealth. They can make sense, though, as a way to manage your child's savings from a summer job, or to invest relatively modest monetary gifts. You may want to consider using this type of account as a way of teaching your child about investing.

Building a Strategy

11

Saving

By the time they've reached this point reading *other* books on investing, people are usually just getting started. They've waded through words of introduction, a few inspirational anecdotes, some autobiographical information, perhaps the author's favorite recipe, and they're ready to turn to the subject at hand. Clever you, you've already learned that small caps aren't for people with tiny heads and junk bonds aren't for bundling up trash. You've learned about REITs and mutual funds and retirement accounts and you haven't broken a sweat. In short, you've laid down a good base of knowledge. Now you're ready to begin building a strategy.

The first rule for success as an investor: *save*. Unless you inherit a fortune, win the lottery or marry a former Beatle, you'll need a solid program of saving to lay the foundation for the wealth you hope to accumulate. You have to start an investment account of some kind and add money to it on a regular basis.

The point of all this

For some people saving comes naturally. They accumulate wealth without budgeting or any other apparent effort. I put them in a class with people who remain slim without dieting or exercise: alien beings sent to torment the rest of us. Most of us need a good reason to accept delayed gratification.

People of a certain age are likely to have little problem with motivation, as the resources required to meet their retirement needs come into focus. Most of us see a wide gap between the lifestyle we hope to enjoy during those years and the one provided by Social Security. We're hit with the hard truth that among all life's financial needs, retirement is the only one for which you can't borrow.

Younger folks, bless their hearts, are likely to feel less urgency. They may even express some disdain for the enterprise. *Money isn't the most important thing in life*, they'll observe, quite accurately. *You can't buy happiness.*

Yet a sound plan can make a real difference in your quality of life. Financial security is good for your peace of mind. It offers greater freedom of choice about where and how you live, how long and at what job you work. It may permit you to spend more time engaged in whatever artistic or sporting or other pursuit stirs your passion, or simply spend more time with your family. You may gain satisfaction from being able to provide financial assistance to your parents or children, or support your favorite charity.

All these things are easier to achieve when you start saving earlier. We saw in Chapter 2 how the power of compounding works to the advantage of those who invest over a longer period of time. The best time to start a program of saving and investing, or boost an inadequate one, is always the same: *now.*

The anti-investment

We leap into debt, but crawl out. Oh man, how I wince at the thought of the wealth I'd have now if I'd taken that bit of ancient wisdom to heart as a young man.

One of the chief ways to make wealth grow is to receive interest on money we've made available to others. When you incur debt you're doing exactly the opposite. You're paying interest instead of receiving it. You're less financially secure, and more likely to suffer genuine hardship from an event that might otherwise be a relatively minor setback. Borrowing is the anti-investment.

Okay, maybe you need a car before you have enough saved up to buy it for cash. Fine, but in this case you should be buying basic transportation, not the car of your dreams, and definitely not a brand new one that will lose many thousands of dollars in value the day you drive it off the lot.

Few people save the full price of a home before buying one, and that's okay, too. The problem comes when people stretch the limit of what they can afford. Lending policies regained sobriety in the wake of the collapse in housing prices that began in 2008, but you shouldn't assume it makes financial sense to make the most expensive purchase for which you can qualify. Your home should be comfortable fiscally as well as physically.

Do I need to talk about the evils of credit card debt? You've heard about that, right? The same goes for other forms of consumer debt, including the ones that scream, *Pay no interest! Pay no interest!* Hint: the interest charge is built into the cost of whatever you're buying.

If you can't save

People go through periods when saving simply isn't possible. Illness or unemployment may temporarily deprive you of the income required to add to your investments. There's not much we can do about shifting fortunes. Shift happens.

But there are plenty of people who believe they can't save even while they're earning a good living. I spent some of my working years in that mindset, and I know I'm not alone. If you find yourself harboring that thought, bear in mind there are people who earn less money than you. Somehow they manage to get by on a smaller income, so it's clearly possible. Some of them, in fact, are not just getting by, they're adding to their savings. They would roll their eyes at the thought that someone making the kind of dough you're pulling in can't find a way to do the same. Anyone with a reasonable income can save if they make it a priority.

Go robotic

An automatic saving plan can be one of the best things you do for your financial health. It can take a lot of the pain out of saving and, more importantly, take the "forget" out of saving as well. If cash goes directly from your paycheck or bank account into an investment account, you don't have to worry about accidentally spending money you intended to save.

Automatic saving is built into 401k and similar retirement plans. Money that otherwise would have appeared in your paycheck goes directly into your retirement account, un-touched by human hands. Many employers will make direct deposits from your paycheck to multiple accounts, providing a way to shoot money straight into an investment account you set up on your own.

You can also create your own automatic saving plan with many mutual fund companies and other investment firms. You simply give them your checking account information and tell them the amount to pull into your investment account each month. Many of these firms allow you to start an account with a smaller minimum balance if you set up automatic deposits.

These arrangements don't entirely eliminate the need for attention. When your income rises you'll want your savings to keep pace. Review your 401k contributions or other automatic savings from time to time to see if they need a boost.

Dollar cost averaging

When you're buying an investment that fluctuates in value, you face the risk that you'll buy at one of the local peaks, paying a higher than average price. You'd like to do the opposite, catching it in one of the valleys, or "buying on the dip" as people like to say. The zigzags are essentially random, though, and trying to outguess them is a losing game. You could lose the benefit of a nice upswing while waiting for a decline to occur, and when it does, it could be the start of a longer decline rather than a brief dip in price.

Yet there's a way to stack the odds in favor of buying at a below-average price. It goes by the fancy name *dollar cost averaging* (*DCA* for those in the know) but it's so simple that many people do it without realizing. All you have to do is add the same dollar amount to your investment at regular intervals.

Suppose you're socking away $200 per month and investing that money in a mutual fund that fluctuates quite a bit. The first month you buy at $7 per share. Then some kind of excitement makes the price shoot up to $13, the price you pay the second month. The buzz is gone by the time you make your purchase in the third month at $10 per share.

Looking back, you're glad you didn't buy all your shares at $13 and perhaps wishing you could have caught the $7 price for all these purchases. You avoided the extremes, though, buying at three different prices that average out to $10.

Your total investment for these three months is $600, and with an average price of $10 per share you might expect to have bought 60 shares. When you check your account, you're pleasantly surprised to see that you own about 64 shares. What happened? You invested $200 each month, and with that amount of money you bought more shares at the lower price (about 29 shares at $7) and fewer shares at the higher price (only about 15 at $13). The overall result is an average cost of $9.38, even though the average of the three prices at which you bought was $10.

I used the old author's trick of exaggerating the numbers for dramatic effect. Mutual funds don't often go from $7 to $13 to $10 in such a short period of time, so you aren't likely to get quite this big an advantage from dollar cost averaging. Yet it's nice to know you have this added edge when you make regular additions to your investment account. You become something of an accidental genius, always buying fewer shares when prices are high and more when prices are low.

12

Setting Priorities

Okay, you're saving money, now what are you going to do with it? Our main interest here is building wealth through high-quality long-term investments, but first we have to deal with some preliminary issues.

Short-term needs

Serious investing exposes your money to the risk of short-term losses. Money you know you're going to need within the next couple of years should never be exposed to this risk. Examples include tuition for next semester or next year, or cash to cover taxes you're going to owe next April.

Chances are that you'll be disappointed with the growth rate you can achieve with safe, temporary investments of the kind described in Chapter 6. That's nothing compared with the dismay you'll feel if the money isn't there when you need it. The potential for handsome short-term returns always comes with the risk of loss. *Never take risk with money you can't afford to lose.*

61

High-interest debt

I won't insist that you pay off every last stinking dollar you owe on every loan you've ever taken out before you start investing. On the other hand, you should recognize that paying down debt *is* a form of investing. The rate of return is equal to the rate of interest being charged on the debt you eliminate. Best of all, unlike stocks and bonds, it's an "investment" that doesn't expose your money to any risk. Pay off the debt and the interest charges go away, simple as that.

So it doesn't make a lot of sense to make risky investments that might grow at an average rate of 7% to 9% while running a credit card balance that's costing you more than twice as much. Paying down debt is the quicker picker upper.

If your debt repayment plan is going to take a while and you're eager to get your feet wet, I see nothing wrong with starting a *small* investment account, particularly if we're talking about a 401k where you get matching money. Just remember that paying down debt is a higher priority than bulking up your investment account, especially when the interest rate you're paying is higher than the return you can reasonably expect from your investments.

Emergency fund

The conventional wisdom is that everyone should have an emergency fund that's liquid and safe. (It's *liquid* if you can quickly convert it to spendable cash.) Ideally it should be large enough to cover living expenses for whatever time it might take to recover from an accident or illness, natural catastrophe or loss of a job. The gold standard is to be able to cover all necessities—mortgage or rent, utilities, food, taxes—for six months.

That's a worthy goal, but I disagree with those writers who insist you can't begin investing until you've reached it.

Even if you don't have any debts to pay off, it can take years to build an emergency fund to the level where it covers six months of expenses. It seems harsh to keep investments with genuine growth potential off the table throughout that period.

Yes, there's a chance you'll lose some of this stash if you invest it in stocks and bonds, but the probability is that you'll reach the goal of a six-month emergency fund faster if you accept a measure of risk in exchange for faster potential growth. Here's a possible plan:

- First, build a cash fund (in a savings account or money market fund with check writing privileges) that can cover smaller emergencies such as car repairs.

- Next, build your six-month fund using investments that involve moderate risk. You might put up to 30% of this money in a well diversified stock mutual fund, with the rest in bonds or cash. While working toward this goal you'll gain a little experience with the stock market's ups and downs, but shouldn't experience serious setbacks.

- After you've reached this goal and begun to build permanent savings that aren't part of your emergency fund, move toward having the entire emergency fund in cash.

Make sure this money is invested only in items you can cash in quickly at little cost. Don't put it in a traditional IRA because of the taxes (and possible tax penalty) if you tap it. A Roth IRA might make sense for your emergency fund, though, because you can withdraw contributions (though not earnings) at any time without tax or penalty.

13

The Nature of the Game

We've arrived at the heart of the matter, which is how to handle your core investments. We need to identify strategies that will help you reach your long-term goals—and ones you must avoid to minimize the risk of catastrophic failure.

The key issues relate to the stock market. Stocks are the main engine for growth in long-term investing, but also the main source of risk. It's fair to say they're also the main source of misunderstanding, so we're going to learn more about stocks before moving on to build a strategy.

Dangerous cocktail

Much of the investing public would take the following to be a combination of common knowledge and common sense:

> A stock will perform well when the company performs well. If you learn enough about a company to know it's performing well, its stock can be a relatively safe investment. In any event, you can avoid serious losses by keeping a close eye on your stock investments. That's

hard to do when you own many different stocks, so you may be better off owning a few, or even just one if it's a really good stock.

A good mutual fund manager or financial advisor should have a pretty good idea which stocks are going to perform well and which ones to avoid. You can tell how good a money manager is based on his or her track record. If you lose money with one, it's a good idea to switch to another.

When the overall stock market is going down, the smart thing to do is pull your money out and wait for a good upward trend before buying stocks again. Go with the prevailing opinion, buying when people are upbeat about stocks and selling when the public mood turns sour.

This general view of the stock market seems sensible and coherent. It's common among investors in general, including many who are smart and well educated. Yet it's a dangerous cocktail of misconceptions and faulty logic that typically produces inferior investment results while exposing you to excessive risk.

These false ideas are powerful, though. They're constantly reinforced in the media and in what we hear from friends, family and colleagues. Huge businesses are built around the profits that can be extracted from people who accept these notions. You'll find it hard to resist all that pressure unless you develop good habits of thought based on a deeper understanding.

FedEx delivers, Whole Foods doesn't

Let's begin by testing the first statement above, that a stock will perform well when the company does. Consider these routine items from the *Wall Street Journal* describing quarterly earnings reports. One glows with optimism:

> FedEx Corp., lifted by strong gains in shipment volume across almost all its delivery businesses, reported that its fiscal first-quarter profit more than doubled and said it

sees no signs of a letup heading into the peak shipping season.

This one, not so much:

Whole Foods Market Inc. reported that its fiscal second-quarter profit dropped 32% on declining sales and margins. Whole Foods also warned that sales comparisons would be challenging in the first half of the year.

As you might expect, investors were pleased with one of these reports and not the other. But it was the stellar news from FedEx that brought disappointment. Immediately after the announcement, FedEx shares fell 3.9%. On the heels of the gloomy report from Whole Foods, its stock shot up 7.6%.

Knowledgeable investors aren't the least bit surprised to see results like these. Stock prices don't *always* move opposite to the company's performance, but it's a common event. Let's see why.

The auction

As a general rule you can't buy stock directly from the company that issued the shares. If you want to snap up some Kodak, for example, you need to find another investor who already owns that stock and is willing to sell.

That's the whole point of a stock exchange. In essence it's an electronic meeting place for all the people who want to buy or sell shares of the stocks that trade there. When you place an order, your broker transmits it to the exchange where the stock is traded. Computers check for a compatible order from another investor (a seller for your buy order, or a buyer for your sell order). If they find one, it's a done deal, usually completed in less than a second if the market was open when you placed the order.

The price is determined through an auction process. When you buy, you get the lowest price available from investors offering shares for sale, and when you sell, you get the highest available bid. If you want, you can specify the highest purchase price or lowest selling price you'll accept, but then you won't have a deal until your price becomes the best one available. With billions of shares changing hands every day, the whole thing is pretty much like eBay on steroids.

The future is now

One of America's favorite pastimes is trying to "beat the market" by choosing stocks that will perform better than others. From what we've just learned it should be apparent that people playing this game are actually trying to beat *each other*. Whenever one investor gets an especially good deal, buying before a steep increase in price or selling before a collapse, someone else gets the opposite result.

No one wants to get the short end of that stick, so you won't find anyone willing to sell at a low price after it becomes clear the company is doing really well. The trick is to identify companies that are going to perform well (or poorly) before other investors figure it out. Countless investors, many of them professionals, buy and sell based on what they hope will be the earliest and most accurate forecast of a company's performance. The result: *today's stock price always reflects investors' expectations about the future.*

Now we can see the reason for the strange stock market reactions we saw earlier. Ahead of the company's announcement, investors already knew FedEx was on a roll, and the stock price reflected that rosy forecast. The actual results, strong as they were, fell short of expectations, so the stock price skidded. Similarly, investors were aware things at Whole Foods were rotten, and lifted the stock price after learning the company's troubles, though far from trivial, weren't as bad as feared.

Walk this way

Investors put a huge amount of effort into forecasting the performance of companies, industries and the economy as a whole. Professionals managing huge sums for mutual funds, hedge funds and the like have at their disposal smart, hard-working researchers, fast computers, and top-secret software developed at great expense. These pros dominate the market to such an extent that stocks rarely deviate far from prices they consider reasonable.

The result is stock prices that reflect everything that's known about a company's past and present, and everything that can be forecast about its future. When everything that's expected about a company is built into the price of its stock, significant changes in the price will occur only as a result of something unexpected. In other words, changes in stock prices won't be predictable; they'll be largely random.

To be more specific, stock price movements resemble something called a *random walk*. Imagine a drunk staggering from one bar to the next, where he's about equally likely to step forward or backward. A graph of his progress, created using a random number generator, would look like a graph of stock prices. The concept gave Burton Malkiel the title for his best-seller, *A Random Walk Down Wall Street.*

We often see people make predictions about particular stocks or about the stock market as a whole. Sometimes they go so far as to set a target price they think a stock will hit within a specific time period. The forecast may be backed by extensive research and delivered with confidence by an articulate professional in an expensive suit. Yet studies of those predictions find that they're about as likely to be accurate as a coin flip.

Many people find it hard to accept this much randomness in stock prices. If you're still dubious, see if you can find your way out of the *prediction paradox*, which we met briefly in Chapter 3.

The prediction paradox

Imagine that there's a reliable way to predict which stocks will do better than others. Investors can use it to buy stocks that are ready to take off and sell when they're going to disappoint. Do you see the problem? If all investors can use this method, people holding the winners won't sell at today's prices. Likewise, there won't be any buyers for the losing stocks. The predictions will be useless because no one will cooperate with an investor who's trying to gain an advantage.

A method of prediction, even a good one, loses value when it becomes widely known. As soon as the investing public catches on, they adjust their behavior and the method no longer works. The better it is, the more people will use the method, and the more quickly it will lose its effectiveness.

The best-known example is a theory called *Dogs of the Dow*. The Dow Jones Industrial Average is based on the stock prices of 30 leading companies. Although these are among the most prominent businesses in the world, some of them fall out of favor with investors from time to time. These "dogs" will sell at a relatively low price in comparison with their annual dividend.

Someone did a historical analysis of these stocks and found something interesting. Apparently investors had a tendency to become overly pessimistic about these stocks, sending the price lower than the facts justified. Based on past performance, it appeared that investors could achieve excellent results with a simple approach of buying the least popular stocks in the Dow, as measured by dividend yield.

The theory received a lot of publicity—it was the subject of a best-selling book—and many people adopted the approach. As more people bought these stocks, the prices didn't drop as low. The opportunity to profit from a rebound disappeared, and these stocks no longer performed better than average. When Dogs of the Dow became widely known, the prediction paradox made it useless.

J.P. Morgan, the leading financier of his time, was asked to predict what the stock market would do, and all he could say was, "It will fluctuate." Warren Buffett, perhaps the greatest investor ever, once remarked, "I can't predict the short-term movements of the stock market. I haven't the faintest idea as to whether stocks will be higher or lower a month—or a year—from now." The prediction paradox spares no one.

Like playing cards

Investing isn't like chess, where the outcome depends solely on the skill of the players. Randomness affects the results, so it's more like a game of cards where you lose some of the time even with perfect play.

In a card game you might have two ways to play a hand, one that wins two-thirds of the time and another that wins only when the first one doesn't. Good players choose the play with a higher probability of success. They stick with the better play even when it fails several times during a run of bad luck.

The same is true in investing. Over the next few chapters we'll cover the key principles that shift the odds in your favor. They'll allow us to build a strategy for long-term success. That strategy won't win all the time, though. You'll go through periods when a different way of investing that's normally inferior produces better results. The high level of randomness in investing prevents us from predicting when these periods will occur, so smart investors stick with a good strategy even when the results are disappointing.

This is harder than it sounds. Card players can draw the line between luck and skill. They don't kick themselves for having failed to predict that the next card would be the jack of spades. Investors swim in an ocean of information with currents flowing in all directions. When things go wrong, hindsight always reveals warning signs we failed to heed. Bad luck masquerades as bad strategy.

Don't fault yourself (or your advisor) for failing to foresee the unforeseeable. Wise investors know that even the best strategy produces bad results some of the time. They don't abandon a good strategy during these periods.

14

The Right Stuff

There are four rules for investment success that are more important than any others. The first, covered in Chapter 11, is to maintain a regular program of saving. Now you're ready for the second: maintain an appropriate division of your money among the different classes of investments. Some people refer to this process as diversification, but we're going to reserve that term for the different issue of how you spread your money around *within* each class of investment. We'll use the more specific term *asset allocation* for the focus of this chapter. The main question here is what percentage of your money should be invested in stocks as opposed to bonds or other investments.

A famous study looked at a number of pension funds to determine what factors were most important in making some of them perform better than others. Surprisingly, skill in selecting particular investments had only a small effect. Likewise, skill in choosing when to invest based on whether the stock market was expected to go up or down was of little value. Nearly all the difference in performance came from the funds' policies regarding asset allocation—the percentage of the fund that went into each of the different classes of investments. That's an amazing result when you consider all the effort people put into trying to figure out how particular stocks, or the overall stock market, are going to perform.

We'll assume for now that the only kinds of investments you need are stocks and bonds, and talk about how to divide your money between those two. Keep in mind that we're talking about your permanent investments. Your emergency fund or any money set aside for a near-term purpose should be excluded from this process.

All or nothing

It may seem logical that all your money should go into whatever category is best. Yet there are powerful reasons to maintain a mix of stocks and bonds.

The prediction paradox we met earlier prevents us from knowing which will do better in any particular period of time. If investors had some way of knowing stocks would outperform bonds, for example, no one would buy bonds at their current price. Bond sellers would have to sweeten the deal until stocks no longer had a clear advantage. So the first problem with going all or nothing is that we can never know which category will perform best.

A portfolio that contains a mix of stocks and bonds gains an edge from the way the two types of investments interact. Bonds can perform well at the same time stocks are tanking, and vice versa. These offsets produce a special benefit when you hold both together. If you add bonds to an all-stock portfolio, your return may go down, but risk goes down much faster. Likewise, when you add stocks to an all-bond portfolio, return goes up faster than risk. The blend is your friend.

There's a simpler reason to avoid going all-or-nothing. If all your money is in bonds, it may not grow fast enough to meet your goals. And if it's all in stocks, you'll be exposed to too much risk. How much is too much? We'll get to that, but first we need to look at another way common sense may mislead you.

Formula for failure

It seems logical that you can do better than average in the stock market if you pull your money out when it's going

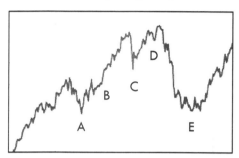

down and reinvest when it's going up. Let's see how that would work during a period when stocks perform like this.

You begin happy enough, going up and up, but then there's a setback. It looks like the market is going down, so you sell at point A. That was bad luck, because prices were just about to turn upward, but you had no way of knowing that. You wait for a good upward pattern to develop before buying again at point B, losing all the profit you could have had between those points. The same thing happens again when you sell at point C and buy at point D. Finally you learn your lesson and decide not to sell until there's a bigger decline. Using that approach you sell at point E and miss the sharp rebound afterward.

Comparing the right side of the chart with the left, we can see what a sweet result you would have had if you simply held on throughout this turbulent period. The idea of selling when the market goes down cuts into your profits and may even leave you with a net loss. This common strategy is a formula for failure. It forces you to hold stocks during at least part of a downturn (until you decide the market is heading down) and miss at least part of an upturn (until you figure it's heading up again).

The real problem here is in the underlying notion that recent movements tell us which direction the market is moving. The only thing they really tell us is which direction the market *was* moving. The next move is always unpredictable. Selling during a stock market decline often produces a pattern like the one here, where the investor fails to avoid losses but succeeds brilliantly in reducing profits.

For best results you have to fight the urge to abandon the stock market when it goes down. That's hard to do when you see your account balance shrink and people around you are saying this is a bad time to hold stocks. But that's precisely when it's *best* to hold stocks. When other investors are filled with fear, stock prices are lowest and the potential for profit is highest.

It's about time

There are two big factors that determine how you should divide your money between stocks and bonds. One is the length of time between when you make the investment and when you expect to use the money. Money you expect to use next year, or even a few years from now, shouldn't be in the stock market. It might grow handsomely during that period, but the reverse is also possible. Each time the market takes a tumble we hear sad stories of people who gambled and lost with money they'd set aside for next year's college tuition. Instead of the education they were planning, they get a hard lesson in economics.

Stocks make sense when your time horizon is longer. You'll still experience setbacks, but you'll have time to recover from them. The overall faster growth associated with stock investments means the odds of getting a poor result get smaller and smaller when we look at longer time periods. Are you saving for retirement? Putting money into a college fund for your three-year-old? Sensible stock investments can help you reach these goals if you have the discipline to tough it out during bad patches.

It's about you

And that's the other big factor in determining your asset allocation: your ability to ride the ups and downs of risky investments without a severely upset stomach. Risk tolerance is partly a quality of life issue, because you can't be happy when you're consumed with worry about losing money. It's also a strategic issue, because you won't be able to stick with a plan that takes you too far outside your comfort zone. In all likelihood you'll abandon the strategy just when it's most important to stay the course, dealing your finances a major blow.

Many people overestimate their appetite for risk. They focus on the higher returns that go with risky investments and give too little thought to the losses they might suffer. It can be hard to judge how you'll react when you see your account value plummet.

Financial advisors sometimes try to assess their clients' actual risk tolerance by having them answer a series of questions that might include one like this:

> Suppose you made an investment and six months later it had lost 25% of its value. How would you respond?
>
> A. Sell before it loses more value
>
> B. Hold on, hoping it will recover
>
> C. Buy more, hoping to benefit from the lower price

There is no right or wrong answer to this question. Its purpose is to get a better picture of what strategy best fits your personality. Do you really have a strong tolerance for risk? Or just a strong tolerance for profits?

Rule of thumb

You may be wondering what the experts recommend for a normal kind of person, Joe the Investor, if you will. Ask around and you'll get a range of answers. Some advisors say you should own your age in bonds and put the rest in stocks. For example, if you're 35, you would hold 35% in bonds and 65% in stocks. More aggressive advisors suggest increasing your stock percentage by ten or more points above that level if your risk tolerance is strong.

I suspect that much of the disagreement has to do with a disconnect between the level that would be ideal for someone with a strong risk tolerance and the level that's bearable by the typical investor. Experts who recommend the higher stock percentages may be right in the sense that someone who's able to stick with that approach through thick and thin will likely end up with a better result. Yet those higher stock percentages will produce deeper losses in a bear market, leading many investors to crash and burn, selling their stock holdings at the worst possible time. To put you on a path you'll find easier to follow we'll use the rule of owning your age in bonds as the default.

Consider dialing back your stock exposure if you're carrying a lot of debt. Bond investments make you a lender who receives interest, so you're cancelling some of your bond investments when you do the opposite, borrowing money and paying interest. On the other hand, you might consider reducing your bond fraction if you have steady, low-risk income from other sources such as social security or a pension, because having a right to receive this kind of income is similar to owning a bond.

There are other factors that might affect the decision. How much growth do you need to meet your goals? What do your health and family history say about your likely longevity? It's a question that requires a judgment call, but you may want to think twice before straying far above or below the base recommendation of owning your age in bonds.

Rebalancing

When you invest a certain percentage of your portfolio in stocks, you can't expect that ratio to remain the same. It will change depending on whether stocks are doing better or worse than other investments. The process of restoring your portfolio to the previously targeted ratio is called *rebalancing*.

Presumably you had good reasons for the allocation you created, and returning to that allocation is part of the reason for rebalancing. This process produces a side benefit, though. It causes you to buy more stocks after a sharp decline, and sell some (or buy less) after a steep rise. That's exactly what you want to be doing: buying low and selling high. In theory at least, rebalancing should help you achieve stronger returns.

Studies of how rebalancing works in practice have not shown uniformly positive results. It appears that rebalancing too frequently, or when deviations from your target percentages are small, can actually reduce your returns. It probably makes sense to rebalance once or twice a year, and skip it when you're within a few percentage points of where you want to be.

In any event you should keep costs in mind. In particular, you should be reluctant to rebalance by making a sale that will incur a significant tax liability. In a situation like that it may be better to rebalance gradually by pumping up your savings in the category that's underweight.

You have to expect that some of the time the stock market's next move after you rebalance will make you wish you'd left well enough alone. You might shift money from bonds to stocks to rebalance after a decline in the market and then see—*ouch!*—a further drop in stock prices. When that happens you may be tempted to think this is a poor strategy.

In dealing with events that are fundamentally unpredictable, though, it's never a mistake to choose the course that gives you the best odds of success. In the long run, rebalancing is a winning strategy.

15

Diversification

Rule #3 (handwritten)

Our third rule for success is to make sure your investments, especially your stocks, are well diversified. This may be the single most important principle of investing, but also the most misunderstood. Many people think this is a platitude about not keeping all your eggs in one basket, designed to help incompetent investors avoid hurting themselves too badly. *I'm smart enough to keep an eye on a stock and make a good judgment about when to sell,* they think. Meanwhile they believe that focusing on one stock, or a few, will help them grow wealthy. *If I diversify, my investments won't grow as fast.*

Wrong on both counts. Diversification is essential for *all* investors. It's the centerpiece of a good strategy because it provides a way—the *only* way—to reduce risk while maintaining the same rate of growth. It's like wearing a seatbelt, helping you avoid serious injury without slowing you down.

This topic provided one of the main motivations for this book. Nearly all books on investing recommend diversification, but many of them fail to emphasize its importance. Shorter ones designed for general audiences rarely take the time to explain how it works. I'm hoping to persuade the doubters by offering a condensed version of what you might learn if you undertook a serious study of investing.

Before we move on, though, let's be clear about how we're using the word. Some people say they're diversifying when they divide their money between stocks and bonds. That's a legitimate use of the word, but for our purposes that's a separate issue, covered in the previous chapter. This chapter is about what happens *after* you've made that division. How are you going to handle the money you've decided to invest in stocks? Will you keep it concentrated in a few stocks, or maybe just one? Or will you be wise enough to diversify broadly?

We'll begin by understanding that you can't manage risk by keeping a close eye on a stock investment. Then we'll look at how diversification reduces risk—and does that without slowing the average rate your investments grow. We'll finish up with some words for people who want to keep a big chunk of their money invested in stock of the company where they work.

Dumb beast

We're used to the notion that we can manage risk by staying alert. It's an idea that serves us well in potentially dangerous activities like driving, or dating. It doesn't work with stocks.

To avoid losses you would have to know when the stock was about to go down, and sell before that happened. The implicit assumption is that the stock market is some kind of dumb beast that will absorb shares at today's price even when a brainy person like you can see that the stock is heading south.

In reality, today's price can be where it is only because investors—including the professionals who dominate the stock market—are willing to pay that price. They won't do that if there's some way to know the stock is about to become cheaper. It's that pesky prediction paradox again: if there were some way to know the stock was going lower, it would *already* be lower.

Short-term stock movements are random. Keeping a close eye on a stock won't tell you when it's about to go down, any more than watching a roulette wheel will tell you when to switch from red to black.

Reducing risk

Imagine that you've identified ten stocks as candidates for your portfolio. You can put all your money in one or divide it any way you like among two or more. It's reasonable to expect that some of these stocks will perform better than others, but we have no way of knowing ahead of time which will be the winners.

Betting everything on a single stock exposes you to the possibility of choosing the worst of the ten. If that happens you'll suffer the worst possible result from any investment in these stocks. It's the riskiest approach.

Dividing the money between two stocks improves your odds. The worst you can do is select the two that perform most poorly and get the average between the two, which will be at least somewhat better than getting the performance of the one that comes in dead last. What's more, the odds of picking the two worst (1 in 45) are smaller than the odds of picking the single worst (1 in 10). You've improved your worst case, and also made it less likely that you'll get the worst case.

The approach with the smallest risk is to divide your money among all ten stocks. You're assured of holding the best of these ten in your portfolio. You'll also hold the worst, but the potential for loss is minimized when your portfolio also holds stocks that will perform better.

The risk for a diversified portfolio isn't simply the average of the risk for each of the stocks. Because of the smoothing effect when different stocks perform well at different times, portfolio risk is lower than the average risk of the stocks. The risk of an individual stock can be two or three times as high as the risk of a portfolio holding many similar stocks.

Sometimes the overall stock market goes down, so you can't eliminate risk altogether even if you divide your money among thousands of stocks. Yet offsetting the bad performance of some stocks with the better performance of others reduces the damage when the market turns sour. Returning to the seatbelt analogy, you can still have an accident, but you're less likely to be badly hurt.

Preserving profits

One of the first things we learn about investing (in this book, anyway) is that risk and reward go together. If you want investments that grow faster, you have to be willing to take more risk. Does this mean you'll get slower growth when you diversify?

No! This is what's truly spectacular about diversification. When we own ten stocks instead of one, the portfolio will grow at the same rate as the individual stocks. If each individual stock was expected to grow at 10% on average, the portfolio will also be expected to grow at that rate. Yet the risk level for the portfolio is much lower than for any of the stocks.

This is a profoundly important result. The added risk that comes from putting too much money in a single stock is called *concentration risk*. It's a particularly ugly kind of risk because it doesn't help your money grow. To use a fancy term from the textbooks, it's *uncompensated* risk.

Admittedly, the diversified portfolio won't grow your money as fast as if you were somehow able to choose the best of those ten stocks. Remember, though, you'll never be able to base that choice on anything more solid than a hunch. The stock wouldn't be trading at today's price if there were a reliable way of knowing it will perform better than others. Whatever advantage you might gain from your insight into the stock's likely performance pales in comparison with the advantage of diversification.

Far and wide

Good diversification isn't simply a matter of dividing your investments among a large number of stocks. You need to hold different *kinds* of stocks. Most importantly, you need to hold stocks in different sectors of the economy, even if you're mainly interested in one particular sector, such as the one in which you work.

Here's an example. During a particularly ugly 2½-year period beginning in March 2000, the Dow Jones Industrial Average, consisting of 30 stocks, fell more than 30%. During the same period, the Nasdaq composite index, consisting of over 2,000 stocks, fell more than *80%*. This huge disparity occurred because the Nasdaq is heavily loaded with technology stocks, the ones that were hit worst in the bear market. The Dow includes technology stocks, too, but also includes McDonald's and Citigroup and Disney and Wal-Mart, stocks that held up a lot better while stocks like Intel were getting hammered. The Dow has fewer stocks, but it reflects the overall economy better than the Nasdaq, so it provides better diversification.

This is a good place for some comments on technology stocks. Fascination with these stocks has existed for hundreds of years. The idea of wealth generated by some powerful innovation—railroads, radio, aviation, the Internet—has a powerful grip on our psyche. This turns out to be good for society as a whole (we get the benefit of the new technology) but not so good for investors.

Technology stocks are frequently overvalued. Over and over we see bubbles in which prices rise to unsustainable levels, followed by debacles in which many people suffer heavy losses. Even in calmer times these stocks may bear prices that aren't fully justified by the companies' earning potential. Studies by experts show that the overall performance of technology stocks is no better than for other stocks. Don't fall in love with this sector; it will break your heart.

Your company's stock

The most frequent choice among people who don't diversify is stock in the company where they work. The company's 401k plan may make it convenient to buy and hold that stock. You may also obtain shares as a result of receiving stock options or restricted stock awards or some other form of equity compensation. The stock seems safer than others because you have a direct view of the company's operations. Working there, you hear plenty of good things about the company.

As a result, many people load up on their own company's stock. The idea may seem to make sense, but consider this: employees are doing the same thing at every other company. They can't all be right in thinking that the stock of their own company is a particularly good investment.

Some experts stress that stock in the company where you work is the single *worst* choice for an investment. One of your most important goals as an investor is to avoid piling one risk on top of another. When your company's business turns sour you may not get the raise or bonus you're expecting, or you might even lose your job. If the company is a major employer where you live, its troubles could affect the local economy and reduce the value of your home. The last thing you need when all that is happening is a major hit to your portfolio. If you're going to load up on one company's stock, it should be a different one, in a different industry, not the one where you work.

I'm not inclined to be dogmatic on this point. Your investments are not just a bunch of numbers. They're a part of your life that can produce wealth and worry and in some cases satisfaction. If I worked for a company with publicly traded stock, I'd want to participate financially in the success I'm helping to create. By holding shares I can also demonstrate loyalty and faith in the company. These are legitimate reasons for holding stock in your company—up to a point.

Where do you draw the line? Experts don't agree on any particular number. The best guideline I've heard is simply this: the amount of money you invest in a single stock should never be more than an amount you can afford to lose. How much is that? Use your own judgment, but be realistic. Chances are that losing 5% of your wealth won't have much impact on your standard of living, but a loss of 10% or more could close some doors you'd like to keep open.

That's too conservative, you may be thinking, *my company's stock will never go all the way to zero.* Well, many people have thought the same thing only to see the stock do exactly that, or come close enough so the difference didn't matter. Meanwhile, the considerations mentioned earlier about piling one risk on top of another make a strong case for prudence. So ask yourself how much you can afford to lose. An honest answer will tell you the absolute maximum you should invest in any one stock, including the company where you work.

16

Expenses

Rule #4 (handwritten)

Our fourth and final rule for success: minimize investment expenses. I can just imagine the excitement you feel at the thought of reading about this glamorous topic. Yet we would need this chapter even if it were not so fascinating. An anecdote from a book first published in the 1940s illustrates the importance.

> An out-of-town visitor was being shown the wonders of the New York financial district. When the party arrived at the Battery, one of his guides indicated some handsome ships riding at anchor. He said, "Look, those are the bankers' and brokers' yachts."
>
> "Where are the customers' yachts?" asked the naïve visitor.

Fred Schwed, Jr. took the title of his hilarious book from the punch line. More than a half-century later, *Where Are the Customers' Yachts?* continues to amuse and instruct its readers on the vagaries of Wall Street, including the ways its denizens transfer wealth from customers' pockets into their own.

Many investors incur unnecessary expenses on the order of two percentage points per year or more. These expenses go

2% of exp - best to avoid (handwritten)

a long way toward explaining why the bankers and brokers have yachts while their customers do not. Remember, an increment of this magnitude can cut in half the amount of wealth you accumulate in a lifetime of investing ("Magnifier effect" in Chapter 2). If this topic doesn't seem sexy enough, pretend this chapter has a different title: *Double Your Money.*

Investment expenses are everywhere—just look at all the money you spent on this book! Some are easy to see, others require some digging, and yet others are invisible (but no less real). We'll start by looking at what happens when you buy and sell stocks in your own brokerage account. Then we'll see how you can cut back on some expenses, but incur others, when you invest in stocks through mutual funds. We'll consider ways of investing that add more layers of expenses, and then, in the following chapter, turn to everyone's favorite expense, taxes.

Trading stocks

A brokerage account allows you to build your own portfolio of stocks. You decide when to buy or sell shares, which ones and how many. Before trying this approach you should be aware of the costs.

Commissions. Brokerage commissions, the most obvious cost, are much lower than they were years ago, before we had discount brokers and Internet trading. They're still far from trivial. You need to think in terms of a *round trip*, because you pay a commission on the sale as well as the purchase. If your broker charges $10, for example, your total commission on a purchase and sale will be $20. That would be a 1% hit against your results from a $2,000 purchase—say, 100 shares of a stock trading at $20. Unless you're quite wealthy, though, you'll have to buy a lot less than $2,000 worth of each stock to create a well diversified portfolio. If you're buying $1,000 worth of each stock, the round trip costs 2%.

Spreads. Many people with brokerage accounts are unaware there's another cost of trading produced by the way stock exchanges work. At any given time, the price at which you can buy a stock is higher than the price at which you can sell. The difference, called the *spread,* (or sometimes the *bid-ask spread*) can be as small as a penny, but it varies from one stock to another and from one moment to the next as orders to buy and sell flow through the stock exchange. Stocks with the largest trading volume have the smallest spreads because so many investors are competing to buy and sell. The lower trading volumes seen for smaller or less popular companies can produce spreads equal to 1% of the stock's price—or 2%, or more. Unlike the commission, the spread doesn't become less significant when you make larger purchases.

This expense is invisible because it disappears into the price at which you buy and sell. Let's walk through an example. Suppose you buy a stock when the best purchase price is $15.00 and the best selling price is $14.85. In this situation you have to pay $15.00 for your shares. You hold the stock for a while, and by coincidence the exact same prices are available when you decide to sell. That means you get $14.85 on the sale. Looking at your brokerage statement, you might think the stock went down 1% because you bought at $15.00 and sold at $14.85. In reality the stock's price hasn't budged. It had to go up 1% for you to break even.

Your broker isn't hiding anything and isn't to blame for the spread. This is just a fact of life about stock market investing, and it can be an expensive one. Brokers sometimes offer promotional deals where you get a number of free trades if you'll open a new account. Those trades aren't really free. You won't pay commissions, but the spreads could cost you hundreds of dollars.

Does this make sense for you? Most people who open brokerage accounts hope to beat the market—in other words, choose stocks that will perform better than average. Yet statistics show that the average performance of retail brokerage accounts is far below the average performance of the stock market. Costs of trading are a big part of the reason.

The expenses of investing through a brokerage account can be reasonable if you hold your stocks for long periods. A round trip that costs 2% (two commissions and the spread) isn't so bad for a stock you hold six years. For a stock you hold six months it's a deadly 4% per year. Unless you have the patience and discipline for long-term investing, these costs can eat most of your profits, or even turn them into losses.

In any event, you're unlikely to buy enough different stocks in a brokerage account to produce good diversification. If you choose this form of investing, it should be just part of the larger picture. Most of your money should go into mutual funds.

Mutual fund expenses

Mutual funds make it possible to obtain the diversification you need at a reasonable cost. They vary widely in their expenses, though. Some take dainty sips from your account, while others guzzle down a large chunk of your profits. Not surprisingly, a number of studies have found that investors generally do better when expenses are lower.

Price of admission. Like any other business, a mutual fund company has to attract customers. Some do that by paying a form of compensation, similar to a sales commission, to the person or firm that persuaded you to make the investment. Payments called *loads* can be made at the time you invest or later, when you sell your shares. Another kind of payment called *12b-1 fees*, named for a controversial regulation permitting them, is paid annually.

These costs are figured as a percentage of the amount invested, and they come out of your pocket. You might, for example, pay a 5% load on a $40,000 investment. If so, $2,000 of your money went to the advisor or firm and only $38,000 went into your mutual fund account. You're permanently deprived of that $2,000 and all the investment earnings you might have received on that money.

You could instead buy a *no-load fund*. As the name suggests, these funds won't extract a sales fee from your account when you invest or when you sell your shares. A fund is allowed to call itself a no-load fund while charging a small 12b-1 fee, but many charge none at all.   *NICE*

Why pay a load when no-load funds are available? I suspect many people who do this have misconceptions about the nature of the payment. They may believe this money is used to hire more talented managers for the mutual fund. Or perhaps they believe it's the price of admission to an exclusive club whose members enjoy superior investment performance. Wrong and wronger. The money is used to pay a sales commission, not to hire genius managers, and studies consistently find that no-load funds perform as well as load funds.

There is one legitimate reason for paying a load when investing in a mutual fund. Advisors who recommend these funds may provide valuable services while charging lower fees than normal, or no fees at all. In a later chapter on working with an advisor we'll see why it might be better to pay for these services directly in the form of fees rather than indirectly in the form of sales loads.

Expense ratio. Mutual funds incur various operating expenses, including management fees and general overhead. The fund's *expense ratio* tells what percentage of the fund's assets is being used to cover these expenses. In theory, a higher expense ratio might be justified as the cost of hiring more talented managers who will boost the fund's performance. Yet many studies have found just the opposite: as a group, funds with lower expense ratios outperform their pricier competitors.

Trading expenses. You can buy mutual fund shares without paying commissions or spreads, but the fund itself will incur these costs when it buys and sells shares. They may be in a better position than you to minimize these costs, but they can't eliminate them entirely. Rapid turnover of stocks can be a drag on the fund's performance.

Bottom line. Focusing on mutual fund costs can make a big difference in the amount of wealth you build over the long term. The easiest way to minimize these expenses is with an indexing strategy as discussed later. Whether or not you use that approach, you shouldn't invest without learning the expense ratio. You should be able to find this number on any financial website that offers information about mutual funds, or in the "Shareholder Fees" section of the fund prospectus. It's hard to justify an expense ratio of much more than 1% for a stock fund when there are index funds that cost less than one-fourth of that amount. You need to be even stingier when buying bond funds, looking for an expense ratio below 0.5%. Funds charging more will occasionally outperform their peers, but over the long run most of them will lag behind, often quite badly.

401k expenses

There's a dirty little secret about 401k plans: many of them—not all, but many—have excessive expenses. What's worse, it's often hard to tell how much expense you're bearing. Sometimes even the company that maintains the plan doesn't know. When this book went to press, the Labor Department was working on rules for better disclosure, but some in the investment industry are lobbying to weaken the proposal.

Meanwhile, disclosure won't necessarily correct the practices that result in these high expenses.

One problem is offering only (or mainly) high-expense mutual funds for the investment choices. As we've just seen, a mutual fund's expense ratio can be a key factor in determining how well it's likely to perform. Making matters worse, at some companies the administrative expenses of the 401k plan get folded into the expenses charged by the mutual funds in your account. It's perfectly legal to charge the plan's expenses against participant accounts, but this arrangement means you're paying the financial firm an undisclosed amount to run the plan for the company.

Problems here are rarely bad enough to turn the 401k plan into such a bad deal that you shouldn't invest, especially if you get matching contributions. Many plans could use improvements in this area, though, especially if they don't currently offer low-cost index funds. If your company's 401k plan doesn't offer high-quality, low-cost investments, an IRA may be a better place for your money.

ETFs

We met the *exchange-traded fund*, or *ETF*, in Chapter 8. Recall that you buy shares of these funds on the stock exchange instead of buying them directly from the mutual fund company. That means you get hit with brokerage commissions and spreads you would otherwise avoid. In theory, an ETF can operate at lower cost than a comparable mutual fund, but it isn't clear these efficiencies translate into better performance. For the typical investor, the added trading costs will exceed any advantage you might hope to achieve, so most of us are better off in traditional mutual funds.

Variable annuities, variable life

If you've read Chapter 9 (and I can't understand why you would have skipped such a charming little chapter), you won't need more than a brief reminder here that variable annuity and variable life policies often (though not always) come with toxic levels of expense, much of it hidden. Putting a large fraction of your wealth in one of the more expensive products could be a mistake that undoes much of your effort in creating that wealth. Use caution, take your time, and when in doubt seek a second opinion from someone who won't profit from the sale.

17

Taxes: This Won't Hurt a Bit

A remark made by old-time TV personality Arthur Godfrey perfectly sums up my attitude toward taxes. *I'm proud to be paying taxes in the United States,* he said. *The only thing is—I could be just as proud for half the money.*

Taxes can be the biggest cost of investing, so this is one of the expenses you have to minimize. Full coverage of this topic would require a book several times the length of this one, so we're just going to cover the main things everyone needs to know about taxation of investments. I promise, this won't hurt a bit.

Help from Uncle Sam

The law offers a variety of ways to get favorable tax treatment for investments. Retirement savings can go in a 401k or IRA (traditional or Roth), and college savings can go in a Coverdell or 529 account. The tax benefits of using these accounts can make a big difference in the amount of wealth you build over a lifetime of saving and investing.

We covered these accounts in Chapter 10. If you're having a hard time choosing, here's the typical order of preference for retirement savings. Begin with your 401k account if you receive matching money. If you don't have access to a 401k plan, or you don't get a match, or you're able to save more than the maximum amount that qualifies for the match, the next best for most people is a Roth IRA. Ideally you would max out the Roth and still want to save more in the 401k even without the match. The tax benefits become greater as you increase the size of the account and the length of time the money stays there, so the basic strategy is to stuff as much money as possible into the account and keep it there as long as possible.

The most common mistake people make with retirement savings, and it's a big one, is to cash out a 401k account when leaving a job. Temptation strikes when you suddenly have access to this stash, especially if you're between jobs and watching your checking account shrink. You shouldn't tap this money before retirement except in dire circumstances. Leave it where it is, or roll it to another retirement account— a 401k with your new employer, or an IRA. You'll thank yourself later.

Taxable accounts

If you aren't using one of these special accounts you have a *taxable account*. As we learned in Chapter 10, you have to pay tax each year on earnings in this type of account, even if you don't withdraw those earnings. If you choose reinvestment for your mutual fund dividends these payments will be transformed into additional shares, yet the IRS will expect you to report this income, just as if you took the cash and spent it on something crazy like alpaca yarn.

Interest. Bonds and cash investments (Chapters 5 and 6), whether held directly or through a mutual fund, produce interest that's generally taxed as *ordinary income*—in other words, taxed at the same rate as wages. Unless your tax rate is high enough to justify investing in tax-exempt bonds, there isn't much you can do about this. Does it help to think of taxes as the price we pay for civilization? I didn't think so.

Dividends. Some companies distribute a portion of their profits to shareholders as dividends. We've been through some periods when dividends were taxed as ordinary income, and others when they received more favorable treatment. When this book was written, qualified dividends were taxed at the lower rates that apply to capital gains, and that may still be true depending on when you're reading this and what Congress has done in the meantime.

Capital gains. Here's the fun part. Profit from selling something for more than it cost is called *capital gain*. And of course when you lose money on the transaction it's a *capital loss*. Here's a quick summary of the basic rules:

- Capital gains and losses are divided between short-term and long-term gains and losses. A gain or loss is long-term if the asset was held at least a year and a day.

- Capital losses always apply first against capital gains in the same category (short-term or long-term).

- If capital losses in one category exceed capital gains in the same category, the excess losses are used without limit to reduce capital gains in the other category.

- If a short-term capital gain exists after all capital losses are subtracted, it's taxed at the same rates as ordinary income.

- If a long-term capital gain exists after all capital losses are subtracted, it's taxed at special, lower tax rates.

- If total losses exceed total gains, the excess can be used to reduce other income (such as from interest or wages), but only up to an annual limit of $3,000 (half that if married filing separately).

- Losses that are unused because of this limit carry forward to the next year when you can use them subject to the same rules. If still unused, they carry over indefinitely to later years.

Planning can make a big difference in the amount of tax you pay on capital gains. The number one strategy is simple: if your investment has gone up in value, don't sell it. Wait until you've held it at least a year and a day, so your gain will be long-term. Then continue to hold it until the following year. And the next. Other things being equal, the longer you wait, the better the result.

The nice thing about this tax strategy, apart from its simplicity, is that it's generally a good investment strategy, too. There are times when you need to sell for diversification or rebalancing, but selling without a strong reason adds unnecessary expense. "My favorite holding period is forever," Warren Buffett likes to say. Sounds good to me.

Losses are another story. These can be used to reduce taxes (subject to limits described above), and a loss you can't use this year can turn out to be valuable as a carryover. *Tax loss harvesting* is both an art and a science; you have to make sure the tax benefit outweighs the transaction costs and avoid harmful distortions in your investment strategy. The main thing to understand is that when an investment declines in value, it's generally a good thing, not a bad one, to capture that loss as a deduction.

When trying to harvest losses you need to be aware of the *wash sale rule.* This tax rule prevents you from claiming a deduction when selling shares at a loss if you buy identical

shares within thirty days before or after the date of the sale
that produced the loss.

More information

I adhere to an ethical code that prevents me from mentioning
that I've written several books on taxation of investments. No
such scruples stop me from directing you to Fairmark.com, a
website I maintain, where extensive information on taxation
of investments is available free of charge (and where you can
learn about my other books).

18

Indexing

Index investing is an approach that sounds strange at first—so strange that many people reject it before they have a chance to learn why it makes sense. You may decide an indexing strategy is not for you, but before making that decision you should understand why these statements are true:

- *On average*, people using an index strategy do better— *a lot* better—than other investors.

- It's possible to outperform an indexing strategy, but the vast majority of those who try end up doing worse, not better.

Before we can discuss an indexing strategy we need to know a little about . . .

Stock indexes

A stock index tells us the average performance of all investors holding shares of companies in a particular list of stocks. Some investors will do better than the index and some do worse. The index tells us how much your investment would have gone up or down if you held every share of every company—or if you held the same fraction of each company.

The most familiar index is the Dow Jones Industrial Average. This is the one most often mentioned on the news, the one people are talking about when they say "the market went up 100 points today." Despite its hold on the public psyche, the Dow isn't suitable for index investing, partly for technical reasons having to do with the way it's calculated and partly because it includes only thirty stocks.

The NASDAQ index also gets a lot of play on the news. Its popularity stems from fascination with technology stocks that dominate this index. The heavy slant toward tech stocks means this index can go down twice as much as a more balanced index when the stock market goes through a bad stretch. As a result, it's a poor choice for index investing, giving you higher risk without higher return.

As the name suggests, the S&P 500 index covers 500 stocks. That's fewer than 10% of all U.S. stocks but these are, roughly speaking, the 500 *largest* U.S. stocks. As a result they represent about 70% of the total value of all U.S. stocks, so this index provides a pretty good measure of the overall performance of the market.

Faster computers have allowed the creation of indexes such as the Wilshire 5000 measuring the performance of *all* stocks that are traded on the major exchanges. In theory this index should be more prominent than others because it more accurately reflects the overall stock market, yet it's almost never mentioned in the news. A total market index provides even better diversification than the S&P 500, and there's reason to believe it will provide somewhat better long-term growth.

There are many other indexes to cover foreign stocks or various slices of the U.S. market, such as health care stocks or small cap value stocks. Indexes have been created for bonds, too.

Index funds

An ordinary mutual fund that invests in stocks will have a manager who tries to select stocks that perform better than others. Success in this profession is highly rewarding, so it attracts talented, highly trained workaholics. Supported by smart, hardworking staff and fast computers with custom software, these managers engage in extensive research and analysis using all information that might help them gain an edge. This approach is called *managed* or *active* investing.

Index funds have skilled managers too, but they don't pick winning stocks. They don't even try! Their job is to match the index. Success is defined by how close they can come to matching the average. This is *index* or *passive* investing.

If you think that's a strange idea you're not alone. It seems obvious that any list of stocks will include some that are going to perform better than others. Even if stocks are hard to predict, it seems like there must be a way to do at least somewhat better than average. Yet people who try to beat the indexes do worse, on average, than people who try to match the indexes. This is not mere accident; in fact, it's a mathematical certainty. Let's see why.

The average of those who aren't average

Imagine that we've given an exam to a number of students, and the average score is 85. As it happens, several of the students scored exactly 85. Set them aside and consider what is the average score of all the other students. I hope you can see that it's 85. The average of those who aren't average is the same as the average of everyone.

The same principle applies to the stock market. An index gives the average of all the investors holding stocks that are included in that index. If we remove all the people who exactly matched the index, we're left with all the people who did not. They're all trying to do better than the index, but the only way some of them can do better is for others to do worse. On average, the people who try to beat the index end up doing the same as those who simply try to match it.

That's before taking expenses into account, however. Matching an index is nowhere near as expensive as trying to beat an index. Investors in managed funds are typically paying at least a full percentage point more per year than index fund investors. People who try to beat the index other ways—trading their own brokerage accounts, for example— also incur higher annual expenses than indexers. When we take expenses into account indexers win, and the difference is huge. Every year they beat active investors by billions of dollars. It's a logical impossibility for active investors as a group to beat, or even match, the indexers. Over the long term, low-cost index funds will outpace the vast majority of comparable managed funds.

Some mutual fund companies have chosen to offer index funds without passing along the cost savings, so it isn't safe to assume that all index funds offer low expenses. It's easy enough to find high-quality, low-cost index funds, however. Before investing, compare the expense ratio of the fund you're considering with the expense ratio of similar funds offered by Vanguard and Fidelity, the leaders in this area.

Index investing comes with other advantages besides low costs. It's easy to be well diversified, so risks are lower. Index investors typically pay less tax than other investors because there's less buying and selling in an index fund than in a managed fund. It's a low-stress, high-return way to invest.

Seems like there has to be a better way

To many people, it just doesn't seem possible that the best approach is to give up on even trying to beat the market. Why not pick a mutual fund, or several, that have performed better than average? Seems logical. A baseball player who won the batting crown last year may not lead the league again, but it's a pretty safe bet he'll do better than average this year.

The same notion doesn't apply to mutual funds, though. One problem is that investment results are heavily influenced by luck, making it hard to know which mutual fund managers are truly skillful. A manager can beat the market purely by chance about half the time, and with thousands of funds out there we should expect some impressive-looking results to appear at random. Ask a couple thousand people to flip a coin ten times and the odds are good that twenty or so will get nine heads, and one or two will get ten.

Then again, genuine skill is effective only so long as the manager can use it to find bargains that are being overlooked by others. An insight into the stock market loses its value when others figure out why those stocks are underpriced. This means a fund manager can lose the ability to produce superior results even if they were based on skill.

Another problem has to do with the size of the mutual fund. When it's small, the manager can get a nice boost by buying, say, $2 million worth of an underpriced stock. If the fund is successful, it might attract enough investors to grow ten times in size, but then it would need $20 million worth of that underpriced stock to gain the same advantage. A purchase this big has an impact on the market, creating a temporary bulge that forces the fund to buy shares at a higher price. The more successful a fund is, the bigger it gets—and the bigger it gets, the harder it is to continue that success.

The fundamental problem is our old friend, the prediction paradox. If we had a reliable way of knowing which mutual funds will perform better than others, then all money would go to those funds, and the others would go out of business. We'd be left with a situation where everyone does better than average, but that's impossible. A world where it's easy to pick winning mutual funds is a logical contradiction.

For all these reasons, past performance by a mutual fund is a poor predictor of future performance. To use an academic term, good performance doesn't *persist*. In fact, one year's stellar performers often end up near the bottom the following year. You can't be assured of beating the index, or even shift the odds much in your favor, by investing with a fund that has done well in the past.

Answering the critics

Indexing has its critics, but often what they have to say is misleading. For example, we sometimes go through periods in which more than half the stock mutual funds beat their index. Fans of active management trot out this statistic as "proof" that indexing is an inferior strategy.

Well, you've heard the expression *lies, damn lies and statistics*. This can't possibly mean that active investors in general are doing better than indexers. In theory, actively managed mutual funds could be above average if active investors other than mutual funds are below average, but that's not the main reason this sometimes happens. Usually it's a combination of factors, including these:

- Stock index funds are always 100% invested in stocks, but actively managed mutual funds typically have at least some cash in reserve. On average this is an advantage for index funds, but when the stock market goes down it gives active funds a slight edge.

- Actively managed funds don't invest exclusively in stocks that are in the index that's being used to measure their performance. They may be compared with the S&P 500 index, for example, while investing some of their money in stocks of smaller companies that are not in that index. In a year when smaller stocks outperform big stocks, this fund can beat its index without beating the overall market.

- Saying that most active funds beat the index isn't the same as saying most investors in active funds beat the index. Sometimes several of the biggest actively managed funds falter, producing poor results for hundreds of thousands of investors and making it easier for a large number of smaller funds with fewer shareholders to beat the index.

During periods of stock market turmoil you're likely to hear that this is a "stock picker's market" when it's easier to find bargains. Keep in mind that even in this type of market the average of those who aren't average is equal to the average. If one stock picker is doing better, another has to be doing worse.

Indexing in perspective

Few issues in the world of investing are more contentious than indexing. Devotees of the strategy think of managed investing as a sucker bet, while critics sneer at the notion of guaranteed mediocrity. What's best for you is a matter of opinion.

It's a mathematical fact, however, that on average, index investors outperform others by a significant margin. Most people who try to do better end up doing worse. There is no strategy with a proven track record of beating indexing. What's more, the strategy is favored by some people you might expect to see on the other side. Warren Buffett, who's devoted his life to beating the S&P 500 Index, says most investors are probably best off in an index fund. Charles

Schwab, founder of the brokerage firm that bears his name, has said most of his mutual fund money is in index funds.

So here's what I recommend. If you're comfortable with the idea, do what I do: put all your long-term money in index funds. If you appreciate the benefits of the strategy but want a shot at outperforming the stock market, do what many other investors do: put most of your money in index funds and a smaller portion in managed funds or individual stocks. And if you just can't accept the notion of putting money in an index fund, remember this: the things you need to avoid are high risk and high expenses. You give yourself the best shot at strong performance if you maintain good diversification and keep your investment expenses as low as possible.

19

Building a Strategy

We're ready to build a strategy, and you may be surprised at how simple it can be. Before getting to specifics, let's review a few high points of what we've already covered.

This strategy is for your long-term savings. It doesn't apply to money you'll need in the near future, which should always be kept in safe *cash* investments described in Chapter 6. Also, although I don't insist on perfectly safe investments for your emergency fund, your risk level for this money should be much lower than for your permanent investments, and you should never put it in a place where you can't cash it out quickly and without serious tax consequences or other penalties.

Step 1: type of account

The first thing you need to figure out is what type of account you'll use for your savings. We covered the choices in Chapter 10. When in doubt, choose a 401k if it's available and offers matching contributions, then consider a Roth IRA if you qualify (you need to have earned income and your overall income must be within limits). Still in doubt? There's nothing at all wrong with a regular, plain vanilla investment account. You can build a retirement account later when your situation becomes clearer.

Step 2: choice of investment firm

Unless your investments are in a 401k or similar plan where you work, you'll have to set up an account to get started. You have plenty of choices, and leading firms are easy to find on the Internet. If you want to make different types of investments you can set up more than one account, though one-stop shopping is available from brokerage firms that offer ways to invest in mutual funds, and mutual fund companies that offer brokerage accounts.

The mutual fund companies best known for high-quality, low-expense offerings are Vanguard, Fidelity and T. Rowe Price. You shouldn't necessarily exclude all others, but keep in mind that a low expense ratio is a better predictor of strong future performance that a recent hot streak.

If you're just starting out you may find that the amount you want to invest is smaller than the minimum deposit, which at some firms is $2,500 or higher. Some firms waive this minimum if you'll set up automatic savings of, say, $100 per month. That's easy to do and a good idea in any event. Still stuck? Open a savings account and stash your money there until it builds to the amount you need for an account at the investment firm of your choice. You're supposed to have an emergency fund anyway, so a savings account is a good idea.

Step 3: saving

A plan for regular saving is the foundation on which you'll build your strategy. Review Chapter 11, especially the part under the heading "Go robotic." Commit yourself to a

program that will add an appropriate amount to your investments at regular intervals, assuring that your savings will be
adequate and securing the benefit of dollar cost averaging.

Step 4: asset classes

Decide how much of your money to invest in stocks, and
how much in safer investments like bonds. This is a key
choice because it determines, more than any other choice,
how fast your money will grow. Selection of winning stocks
or mutual funds—issues that consume much more attention
among so many investors—are far less important than the
basic question of what percentage of your money will be in
the stock market. Review Chapter 14, choose your allocation,
and *stick with it*. Don't let a market plunge scare you out of
stocks, because that's when stocks have the greatest profit
potential.

Balanced funds are mutual funds that have a built-in
division between stocks and bonds. The most common ratio
for these is 60% stocks and 40% bonds, but some of these
funds have higher or lower stock fractions. The beauty of
these funds is that if they stick with the ratio, you don't have
to worry about rebalancing. Remember, though, you'll need
to reduce your stock exposure as you move closer to (or
farther into) retirement.

Life cycle funds, sometimes called *target retirement funds* or
age-based funds, are similar to balanced funds, but are designed
to address the need to change your asset allocation over time.
They automatically cut back on stocks as their investors move
closer to retirement. You choose a fund that's appropriate for
your age or projected retirement date and then forget about it.
The fund will adjust the percentages gradually over a period
of time in a way that makes sense for people your age,
eliminating the need for manual adjustment.

The idea behind these funds is a good one, but their performance hasn't always matched expectations. The fund managers' idea of the right stock percentage for someone your age may not be the same as yours. You may be paying management fees for a stock fund and a bond fund that are included within the target fund, plus an additional management fee just to have someone keep them in the desired ratio. What's more, the stock component may be a managed fund that's more costly and riskier than an index fund. In the stock market meltdown that began in 2008, some target funds lost a lot more value than people would have expected. These bad apples don't necessarily spoil the entire target fund barrel, but you shouldn't assume that a fund based on this good idea is necessarily a good investment.

Do it yourself. Here's a simple approach that requires only a few minutes of your time each year. Decide on the ratio that seems right to you, keeping in mind that the default choice would be to own your age in bonds and hold the rest in stocks. Each year on your birthday check to see how far you are from your target percentage (which is now one point lower than the previous year). If you're within a few points either way, you don't have to do anything. Otherwise, rebalance to your new percentage by moving money from one category to the other, or changing where your added savings will go. Then make a wish and blow out the candles.

Step 5: stocks

There are countless books on how to get the most from your stock investments. In reality there are only two things you have to do: maintain good diversification and minimize expenses. Everything else is far less important.

Some people like to dabble in the stock market, investing a portion of their savings in stocks they've selected. And some like to own stock in the company where they work. That's okay by me, provided you keep your expenses low (avoiding frequent turnover) and never *ever* depart from good diversification for your overall stock portfolio.

Ideally costs should never consume more than one percentage point per year. It can be hard to stay within that limit if you don't use index funds, but low expenses are more important than investing with a fund that produced hot results last year. With index funds you can get below *half* of one percent per year, though you have to pay attention because there are some expensive index funds out there. Whether you're dealing with an index fund or a managed fund, be sure to check the expenses described in Chapter 16. The mutual fund company offers this information in a document called a prospectus, but you may find it more easily on a finance website. You'd like to see an expense ratio as low as possible, and if you're paying a sales load, it shouldn't exceed the value of services you receive from your advisor.

The default choice here would be an index fund designed to match the entire U.S. stock market. Several fund companies have excellent offerings in this category. If this choice isn't available (perhaps because you're investing in a 401k that doesn't offer it), an S&P 500 index fund is a pretty good alternative.

It would be perfectly reasonable to put your entire stock portion into one of these funds. Good diversification doesn't require you to have many mutual funds. You need to invest in many different stocks of different types, and a single fund can meet this requirement. If you want to invest in a fund that specializes in one type of stock, you'll need to own one or more other funds with a different focus to be well diversified.

Many experts recommend putting some of your money in a mutual fund that invests in foreign stocks. Over the long term the growth potential for these investments is about the same as for U.S. stocks. The advantage is getting a smoother ride for your overall portfolio because foreign stocks sometimes do well when U.S. stocks do poorly.

Experts differ on how much foreign exposure is ideal, however. Some suggest that in today's global economy the smartest bet is to balance U.S. stocks with foreign stocks according to their overall value. In this approach U.S. stocks would make up less than half your stock portfolio, because they represent less than half the value of the world's stocks. Others suggest leaning more heavily toward U.S. stocks because the costs of investing are lower, and because a portfolio of stocks valued in pounds or yen may not be ideal for someone who will be living on U.S. dollars during retirement.

Keep in mind that the goal here is to reduce risk by holding assets that may perform well when U.S. stocks falter. Don't leap into a particular country where stocks are on a hot streak because that's often a volatile situation. Spread your money around and invest for the long term. And don't worry if you can't find a way to invest in foreign stocks that fits your situation. Large U.S. companies receive much of their revenue from overseas operations, so you can get a fair amount of exposure to the world economy without investing in foreign stocks.

Step 6: bonds

You'll need to do something with the bond portion of your portfolio. The sweet spot in terms of risk and reward is medium-term bonds, so this should be your main focus. If you're investing in a taxable account and you're in a high tax bracket you should consider tax-exempt bonds; otherwise stick with investment-grade corporate bonds and U.S. treasuries.

The simplest way is to buy shares of a bond mutual fund. Low expenses are even more important here than in a stock fund because the potential for superior returns is smaller. A low-cost index bond fund can be expected to beat nearly all of the more expensive managed bond funds over the long term.

As in the case of stocks, you can own bonds directly instead of through a mutual fund. The best primer on this for general audiences is in *The Only Investment Book You'll Ever Need*, by Andrew Tobias.

Bonds offer lower risk than stocks but can still lose value. As you approach retirement you may want to reduce this risk by putting part of the bond portion of your portfolio in cash or, if you're in a 401k that offers this choice, in a stable value fund.

The most common mistake in bond investing? Chasing after higher yield without recognizing that it comes with added risk. Remember, if a bond investment offers as much return as you would expect from a stock, then it offers as much risk, too.

Step 7: maintenance

A plan like this doesn't need much attention, but you should revisit it at least once a year. The amount you decided to save (step 3) may have been adequate when you started, but needs to ratchet up as your career progresses and your income rises. You also need to check on the need for rebalancing (Chapter 14).

For most people that's all that's necessary. If you've invested in individual stocks or in actively managed mutual funds you'll want to review the results to see if other changes are needed. Are you gaining enough by this approach to justify the added expense, compared with indexing? Have you moved away from good diversification?

Remember, losses will occur with all strategies, so they don't necessarily signal a need to change your plan. The time to be concerned is when results leave you far behind where you would have been if you'd used the simplest possible approach, investing your age in a low-cost bond index fund and putting the rest in a low-cost stock index fund. Deviating too far from those results may indicate you're violating one or more of the cardinal rules. Is your money divided appropriately between stocks and bonds? Are your stock investments well diversified? How high are your expenses?

If you follow these rules you can expect good long-term results despite some occasional setbacks. The main difficulty is mustering the discipline to stick with this program over a period of many years, so we'll talk about that next.

20

Two Demons

Wall Street's oldest truism is that investors act out of fear and greed. Sometimes these emotions spread widely enough to disrupt the financial markets. More importantly for our purposes, they can lead you to abandon a good plan, often at the worst possible time. The greatest danger to your success isn't something in the financial markets. It's right there, holding this book and reading these words. It's you.

Cut me a slice of that

At some point you'll confront what seems like an opportunity to grow your money faster. You may be disappointed with the results of the approach discussed here, or simply bored with it. Meanwhile a different strategy seems like a fast path to riches. Other investors are leaving you in the dust. Worst of all, people with half your brains roll their eyes at what a dope you are for passing up this great opportunity, and you aren't entirely sure they're wrong. If you respond to this impulse, there's a good chance your investments will suffer some serious damage. Here are some of the ideas you need to avoid.

Hot stuff. Once in a while you'll hear that people are getting filthy, stinking rich with some type of investment. Recurring themes include real estate and technology stocks, but there's no end to the possibilities. It may seem odd that tulips sparked investment mania in 17th century Holland, but don't laugh, we had a similar (though more contained) craze for Beanie Babies in the 1990s.

Resist the urge to follow these trends. Simple logic should tell you that good investment results come from buying when prices are low. People who follow a hot trend are doing just the opposite. The worst time to invest in something is when it appears to be going through the roof, because that's when it's most overpriced and poised for a steep fall.

Margin. Many brokers will let you buy shares of stock with borrowed money. This is called *margin* investing, and it's highly profitable—for brokers. Borrowing to buy stock vastly increases the risk without a corresponding increase in return. This is never a good strategy. Oh, and don't borrow on a credit card, or a home equity line of credit, to buy stock or other investments. Bad, bad, bad. Invest with money you save, not money you borrow.

Penny stocks. Companies that don't qualify for trading on the major stock exchanges can still offer shares to the public. These shares often trade for less than $1.00, so they're called *penny stocks.* It's hard to get reliable information on these stocks, and they're frequent targets of abusive schemes. Spreads and other costs of investing tend to be much higher than for regular stocks. In short, this is a lousy way to invest. Remember the old saying: penny stock, pound foolish.

Speculation. There are various ways to speculate on the prices of stocks and other assets. *Day trading* involves buying and selling stocks rapidly, often within the same day. *Commodity options* and *futures* offer ways to bet on the future price of everything from soybeans to silver. *Forex* (short for *foreign exchange*) lets you bet that one currency will gain against another. Each of these ideas can be made to appear as an easy way to get rich. Your money disappears rapidly, though, as you rack up fees for the privilege of trying to outguess the sharks that patrol those waters. You're gambling, not investing, and you can get better odds in a casino.

Options. There are many investment strategies that use stock options, none of them suitable for folks like you or me. The *covered call* strategy gets the most attention. The only thing you need to know about it is this: claims that it boosts your investment return are false. In the long run it does just the opposite.

First line of defense. You can defend yourself against these and similar ideas if you keep in mind one of the fundamental rules of investing: rapid growth and high risk are inseparable companions. When you're offered a way to get rich with little or no risk you can be sure it's a sucker bet. All these ideas can produce good results in the short term, but the same is true for any form of gambling. Stick with what works, and try not to gloat when the results prove you were right.

Protection racket

So much for greed. Fear can be even more powerful and just as damaging. One problem occurs when investors pay for a costly form of protection that drags performance to unacceptably low levels.

Investment firms understand that you would love to get the upside of a risky investment such as stocks without having to worry about losses, so they offer products designed to make it appear this is possible. *Indexed CDs* are certificates of deposit that pay interest based on the stock market's performance while guaranteeing a return of your original investment. Many variable annuities offer similar features.

To profit from these products, sellers have to skim off enough of the upside to make up for any protection they offer against risk of loss. One way or another you pay for this insurance, and in most cases you overpay. The overall performance of these investments is typically poor in comparison with the results you would achieve if you managed risk using the more conventional approach of moving some of your money out of stocks and into bonds or cash.

Losing your balance

Fear can damage your results in another way, prompting you to sell during a downturn. I've explained why this is harmful, but what I can't explain is how to maintain your mental balance while losing your account balance. "Like all of life's rich emotional experiences," Fred Schwed observed, "the full flavor of losing important money cannot be conveyed by literature."

You won't know what a brutal bear market feels like until you've been through one, but I can tell you some of the things that will happen. Many investors will become discouraged with the stock market. Experts appearing on television or in print will reinforce the gloom, pointing out that for the past ten years stock investing was less profitable than yak farming. Many folks will respond by abandoning stocks permanently, while others will cash out with the idea they'll return to the market after the dust settles. All that selling will push stocks even lower. The world of investing becomes an echo chamber: *sell, sell, sell!*

Maintaining an investment in stocks throughout such a period requires a distinct kind of courage. You can't help wondering if the decline will ever end, and feeling stupid for not having sold earlier. It appears that everyone else is heading for the exits while you let the building burn down around you. Yet this is when it is most important to stick with your strategy. *This is the best time to own stocks, because prices are lowest.* The vast majority of those who sell in a bear market end up missing the rewards of the subsequent rebound.

I don't expect you to weather these storms merely because I've told you to do so, any more than a book can make you lose weight simply by telling you to go on a diet and get plenty of exercise. I can offer some ideas, though, that may help you develop good habits of thought.

Prediction paradox. First and foremost, keep in mind that the stock exchanges are places where investors sell shares to each other. The number of shares sold is stubbornly equal to the number of shares bought. If there were a reliable way to predict a further decline in the stock market, there wouldn't be any buyers at today's price. The prediction paradox prevents us from knowing when the famine will turn to a feast.

Take the long view. The stock market's worst falls often come after a steep climb. People tend to measure their losses from the very top of the market, even if they invested at a much lower level. If your account went from $40X to $50X over a period of time, that's an increase of 25%, regardless of how it got there. Don't moan about your losses if the path happened to include an exhilarating trip from $40X to $70X followed by a disappointing fall to $50X.

Reversion. Researchers have found the stock market tends to produce unusually good returns after a period of especially bad performance. They call this tendency *reversion to the mean*, a fancy way of saying that things tend to even out. This is partly due to investor behavior, as they overbuy during the excitement of a bull market and oversell in the despair of a decline. It's also partly due to economic cycles. Easy profits during boom times lead to lax business practices. Low unemployment forces companies to hire less capable workers. Innovation seems less important when old ideas are working well. Inferior businesses survive and continue to consume talent and resources that would be better used elsewhere. For all these reasons, good times carry the seeds of their own destruction. The lean times that follow create the conditions for subsequent success, as poor businesses fail and innovative new ones take their place.

Reversion to the mean is a characteristic of the stock market as a whole but not of individual stocks. You can't expect better than average returns from a stock simply because it recently suffered a steep slide. Part of the stock market's recovery comes from the replacement of some companies with others that compete more effectively.

Be aware also that reversion is a long-term phenomenon. The stock market doesn't always follow a lousy year with a good one. Yet investors with the patience and discipline to hold on long enough have reaped rewards that more than made up for the lean periods.

Contrarian. The best known formula for investment success is just four words: buy low, sell high. Prices are lowest after a severe decline in the market, when investor sentiment is strongly negative and many experts are saying this is a bad time to invest. The highest prices occur when a bull market has lifted spirits, getting more and more people to put more and more money into stocks. Simple logic leads to this surprising conclusion: the best results are reserved for those who do exactly the opposite of most investors. Warren Buffett sums up the key principle as follows: "Be fearful when others are greedy, and be greedy when others are fearful."

Great quote!

Remember this when the market plunges and you hear dire warnings of further carnage. Instead of thinking wow, maybe I should get out while I can, you should realize this is a sign that the stock market is a good place for your money. To earn the richest rewards you need to remain invested during the bleakest times.

What to do when the stock market plummets. *Be afraid. Be very afraid.* Really. Everyone else will be afraid, so there's no reason you should be different. Just make sure you fear the right thing. Most people worry that the market will fall further. Smart investors are afraid of missing out on all the profits to be made in the next bull market. Their greatest fear is that they won't be on board when the train leaves the station.

Helpful bears. Here's one more thought that may help you through a rough patch. Unless we're talking about money you're planning to use within the next few years (which shouldn't be in the stock market to begin with), a decline in stock prices can actually be a favorable development. It never seems that way while it's happening, but years later you could find you have more wealth than if the market had avoided all that ugliness.

When you're adding to your savings and investments, the ability to accumulate more shares of stock at lower prices is a golden opportunity. Continue your regular program of saving and investing, and you'll be buying more shares with each month's savings than before. When the market recovers you'll be ahead of the game.

A decline in stock market prices can help in another way. Many companies continue to pay the same dividend after a price decline as they were paying before. If you're set up to reinvest dividends (which is more or less standard when investing through mutual funds), your dividends will buy more shares than they did at the higher price.

Young people in particular should be positively joyous when the stock market declines. Nothing could be more beneficial to their long-term investment prospects as they get to accumulate shares at lower prices. Most of them don't realize this, and instead moan about the temporary decline in their 401k balances. Perhaps that's just as well: gloating about how they'll benefit from a bear market would make them insufferable to their elders. Remember, though, you lose the benefit of buying shares at a lower price if you bail out when the market takes a dive.

21

Working with an Advisor

Many books on investing point out that advisors cost money and suggest that you can do just as well or better without one. Well, it's certainly true that advisors cost money. One way or another you'll pay for their services. After taking that cost into account, it's unlikely that an advisor will produce significantly better long-term results than you would get if you consistently follow the approach laid out in this book. What's more, setting up and maintaining a good investment strategy doesn't require special skill or a great deal of time and effort. In short, good investing is remarkably easy. *Really?*

Why you may want an advisor

It's easy, though, in the same sense that good nutrition is easy. Knowing you should eat fruits and vegetables and cut back on sugar, salt and fat won't necessarily help you say no to a bacon cheeseburger with fries and a milkshake. Likewise, for all the reasons discussed in the preceding chapter, many people find it hard to stick with a healthy investment strategy.

A good advisor can help you stay on track, shooting down bad ideas and encouraging you to take the long view when the stock market takes an ugly turn. Avoiding a single mistake can save you as much money as you'd likely pay in advisory fees over a period of many years.

An advisor may help you in other ways. You may get an objective assessment of your risk tolerance, something you'll have a hard time providing for yourself. An advisor schooled in asset allocation may fine tune the way your money is divided among different kinds of investments, possibly producing at least a small improvement over the simple strategy described here. Some advisors will produce an analysis of how your program of saving and investment matches up with your retirement plans and other goals, with annual updates so you can make course corrections if needed. Some will look at other aspects of your finances, making suggestions about estate planning or insurance needs. And having an advisor can provide another advantage: many people place value on the peace of mind that comes with having a professional review and monitor their financial situation.

Why you might not

The relationship between advisor and client doesn't always work well, however. Some of the blame lies with clients who have unrealistic expectations. In particular, you shouldn't expect an advisor to shield you from losses. Let me say one final time that you can't earn healthy returns without making investments that will occasionally take a big whack out of your account value. Many people blame their advisors when this happens, but it's a fact of life even with the best strategy.

That's a minor issue, though, compared with the ones sitting on the other side of the desk. There are bad apples in every profession, but quality is particularly uneven among financial advisors. Physicians, lawyers and CPAs all have to meet educational requirements and pass rigorous exams before they can hang out a shingle. A financial advisor doesn't even need a high school diploma. Exams required for certain activities such as being a stockbroker are far too easy to assure genuine competence.

More importantly, many people who call themselves financial advisors would be more accurately called salespeople, and what they have to sell isn't always good for your financial health. They may earn commissions for themselves or profits for their employers by persuading clients to make investments so heavily laden with expenses that inferior performance is virtually certain.

Most advisors who push these harmful products are honest folks who sincerely want to help their clients. They believe in what they're selling and may even have bought some with their own money. The problem is that they've swallowed a heavy dose of biased information that obscures the reality.

There are certainly some high-quality financial products that are sold on commission, and high-quality advisors who sell them. Yet an advisor who receives a commission when you buy one product but not when you buy another has a conflict of interest, making it difficult to be entirely objective in recommending the best possible investments for your portfolio. If you want to avoid this potential problem, you can seek out an advisor who doesn't accept commissions.

Fee-only advisors

A *fee-only advisor* is compensated only with client fees, so that neither the advisor nor any related party (such as the firm where the advisor works) will receive compensation based on sales of financial products. Not all advisors who charge fees qualify: a *fee-based advisor* accepts both fees and commission income. For completely objective advice you need a fee-only advisor.

Some of these advisors charge an hourly rate, while others will quote a fixed fee for a specific service, such as preparing a comprehensive financial plan. Another approach, usually available only after you've amassed a fair amount of wealth, is to charge an annual fee that is a percentage of the amount of money they're managing for you. The key is that they don't make more money by selling one investment instead of another, so they never have an incentive to recommend an inferior product.

Which costs more?

The services of a fee-only advisor may seem expensive, especially when others will advise you without charging a fee. One way or another, though, you'll pay for that no-fee advice, and it may be more costly than you imagine. For example, a $40,000 investment in a mutual fund that imposes a 5% sales load will cost you $2,000. Remember, no-load funds perform as well as load funds, so there's no reason to expect this particular selection to earn back your $2,000 with superior performance. Kiss it goodbye, that money is gone.

The only way to justify paying this load is through the value of services you receive from the advisor. Chances are that you would hesitate to write a check in the amount of $2,000 for those services, yet somehow it seems easier to have the mutual fund company deduct $2,000 from your account and pay it over to the advisor as a commission. And this is another problem in dealing with an advisor who accepts commissions: without realizing it, you may pay much more for the advice than it's worth.

Advisor credentials

Although not required by law, many advisors obtain a form of certification that allows them to put a string of letters after their name. Best-known is the highly respected *Certified Financial Planner* or *CFP* designation, which imposes requirements under four E's: education, examination, experience and ethics. Another strong credential, offered only to certified public accountants with specialized knowledge and experience, is the *Personal Financial Specialist*, or *PFS* designation. There are excellent advisors who don't have either of these designations, but when in doubt this is a good starting point for a search.

The advisor's philosophy

Before agreeing to work with an advisor, ask about his or her investment philosophy. Some accept the wisdom of index investing and others do not. Either way, it's important to work with a professional who will offer advice based on the principles you've learned here: dividing your money appropriately between stocks and bonds, maintaining good diversification, and minimizing investment expense. Advisors who focus on trying to beat the market by selecting winning stocks or mutual funds without regard to expenses are likely to do you more harm than good.

Advisor discretion

Another key question is whether the advisor will be allowed to make changes in your holdings without getting your permission for each change. Generally it's better not to give your advisor this discretion. A good strategy won't involve frequent changes to your account, and when those changes are to be made you should know exactly what is being proposed and why.

22

Closing Words

We've reached the final chapter. That puts me under a lot of pressure, because in just a few minutes you're going to put this book down and you may never pick it up again. Then you'll be on your own, facing the world of investing for a period of time measured in decades. This is my last chance to offer thoughts that may determine whether you achieve long-term success. Here are the things I most want you to remember.

Look at both sides

Every investment transaction has two sides. A great deal for one side is a lousy deal for the other, and no one wants a lousy deal. When an investment looks amazingly good, ask yourself why the seller would offer to enrich you at his expense. Ask yourself why isn't *everyone* buying this investment if it's so great. The better an investment looks, the more likely it is that there's a hidden catch.

The prediction paradox

In a world where transactions have two sides, investments are inherently unpredictable. As soon as people learned of a reliable way to tell which stocks will perform best they would use it to adjust the price they're willing to pay when buying, or accept when selling. At the adjusted price, the stocks would no longer be predictable. Likewise, if we had a reliable way to know which mutual funds will perform best, everyone would flock to those funds and the others would go out of business. All the remaining funds would be above average, but that's impossible.

Ignore the crowd

Resist the urge to follow popular opinion. The best time to buy is when prices are low, and the lowest prices are found when most people (including many experts) are pessimistic. Be wary of today's hot investment, because popularity translates into a high price.

We all lose sometimes

If there were any known way to grow money rapidly without risk of loss, everyone would be using that method and no one would ever suffer losses. No matter what strategy you follow, during a lifetime of investing you're going to endure several periods in which you lose a painfully large fraction of your wealth. You can't avoid losses by switching strategies at the right time, because whatever method you use to determine when to switch is also a strategy, one that everyone would be using if it worked.

Most people who suffer an investment loss figure they made a mistake. Hindsight always reveals warning signs you might have used to avoid the losses. It's hard to accept that losses can occur even when you're handling your investments in the smartest possible way, but that's the truth of the matter.

When you suffer a loss, it doesn't necessarily mean you or your advisor made a mistake. If you abandon a good strategy when it loses money you'll set yourself up for even worse results later.

Four rules for success

Although losses are inevitable, you'll get through those bad periods and achieve good long-term results if you follow these four rules for success:

- First, create and maintain a regular program of saving, in an amount that makes sense relative to your income level and financial goals.

- Second, create and maintain an appropriate division of your money between stocks and bonds, in a ratio that makes sense in relation to your time horizon and risk tolerance.

- Third, within each category of investments, create and maintain good diversification.

- And fourth, keep investment expenses to a minimum.

Disastrous investment results can nearly always be traced to a violation of one or more of these rules. People don't save enough. They shift too much money into stocks while carried away with a bull market, or pull money out of stocks when the market goes down. They put too much money in stock of their own company, or in one type of stocks, especially those glamorous tech stocks, and as a result have poor diversification. They fail to seek out the least expensive mutual funds or annuities, or they rack up trading expenses by buying and selling stocks frequently.

The easiest way to follow these rules is to invest in low-cost index funds. The inherent difficulty of predicting which stocks will perform better, together with the added expense of trying to do so, make it hard to beat an indexing strategy. Use a different approach if you want, but then you'll have to work extra hard to follow these four rules.

Final thoughts

Good investing is simple but not easy. It requires discipline over periods of time that are difficult to imagine—not just months or even years, but decades. At times the temptation to stray from key principles will be strong.

Stick with a good strategy long enough, though, and amazing things happen. You'll learn that you can be just as happy with a lifestyle that lets you add to your savings as when you're spending all your income. Compound interest will work its magic and you'll find yourself holding some serious money. After a number of years you'll see that you dodged a lot of bullets by refusing to give in when speculative investments seemed like an easy path to riches, or when a bear market led so many other investors to sell stocks before a big rebound.

Most of all, you'll have the satisfaction of knowing you did the right thing for yourself and your family. You provided for your retirement and other needs. When things went wrong your savings acted as a buffer, preventing misfortunes from turning into disaster. Having money set aside helped bring peace of mind, gave you more control over your life, and allowed you to be more generous. Investing well took a lot of patience, but it made for a better journey.

Further Reading

One of my goals for this book was to include everything you absolutely need to know about investing. Yet in my zeal for brevity I've omitted much that may be interesting or useful on the topic. Here are some thoughts on how you might add to your knowledge.

Investing in general. For more general knowledge of investing, my personal favorite is *The Only Investment Guide You'll Ever Need* by Andrew Tobias. Crammed with useful facts, common sense and clear explanations, it's also a pleasure to read. The author updates it with new editions from time to time, so it never goes out of date.

I also like *The Bogleheads' Guide to Investing* by Larimore et. al., and Henry Blodget's *The Wall Street Self-Defense Manual.* Fred Schwed's humorous book, *Where are the Customers' Yachts?*, delivers timeless wisdom along with laughs. Two fine books aimed at young adults: *I Will Teach You to Be Rich*, by Ramit Sethi, and *Get a Financial Life*, by Beth Kobliner.

Saving. If you have trouble saving, there are two books that can help you get into the right frame of mind. George Clason's *The Richest Man in Babylon* is an all-time classic, and one of the few money books that outdo this one in brevity. It's a series of parables set in ancient times, emphasizing the virtues of thrift in an entertaining way. One of the stories begins, "In old Babylon there once lived a certain very rich man named Arkad," and goes on to reveal how he became wealthy despite humble origins.

The Millionaire Next Door by Thomas Stanley and William Danko is an engaging look at what the authors learned when they studied actual millionaires. One of the key findings: contrary to their popular image, millionaires tend to be frugal. High-income people who overspend on luxuries often end up accumulating little wealth. The book includes many other observations that might change the way you think about money.

The stock market. For a deeper understanding of the stock market, begin with Burton Malkiel's *A Random Walk Down Wall Street.* He offers clear explanations with the occasional humorous touch. For more on the stock market you'll want to read *Stocks for the Long Run* by Jeremy Siegel, remarkable for the depth and breadth of information it offers.

Most people who invest in individual stocks end up doing worse than if they had put their money in a low-cost index fund. Stock picking can be an engaging hobby, though, and if you keep your trading expenses low and maintain good diversification, you aren't likely to get hurt too bad. Given enough talent and a disciplined approach, you may actually come out ahead, at least if you don't count the value of all the time you put into the effort.

Among the various approaches, the absolute worst is day trading, where you hold stocks for very short periods of time, often selling the same day you bought. Don't waste your time and money on books (or seminars) claiming to teach how to get rich with any form of short-term trading. Nearly everyone who tries it goes broke within just a few months, and some have lost millions.

At the other end of the spectrum, the most respected approach to stock picking is to identify companies that have solid prospects for generating strong profits over a long period of time but for some reason have fallen out of favor with investors. You buy these value stocks with the idea of holding them for years or even decades. If you want to get serious about this approach, begin by reading the books by Malkiel and Siegel mentioned earlier, then read Benjamin Graham's classic *The Intelligent Investor*.

Speaking of intelligent investors, the legendary Peter Lynch offered his thoughts on stock picking in two readable and witty books, *One Up on Wall Street* and *Beating the Street*. Among lesser known books, one that I found interesting is Joel Greenblatt's *You Can Be a Stock Market Genius*, but please ignore his disparaging remarks about diversification and the advantages of indexing.

Mutual funds. The all-time classic in this category is *Common Sense on Mutual Funds*, by John Bogle, founder of the Vanguard Group. He launched the first successful index fund, and his book offers a more thorough explanation of the benefits of index investing than I have given here.

Investment theory. Peter L. Bernstein wrote several readable books on various aspects of investment theory, including *Capital Ideas* and *Against the Gods*. Justin Fox offers a more recent perspective in *The Myth of the Rational Market*. Books by William J. Bernstein (not to be confused with Peter) seek to arm you with the knowledge to turn theory into practice through an approach that focuses on asset allocation. His books keep getting shorter and less complicated, so begin with the latest one, *The Investor's Manifesto*, and if you want to learn more, proceed to his earlier books.

Robert J. Shiller must know how Cassandra felt. The first edition of his book *Irrational Exuberance* warned of a stock bubble and came out in early 2000, just as that bubble was about to burst. A second edition added new information to warn of a real estate bubble, and came out shortly before *that* one burst. Well worth reading but a bit dry for a book with such a juicy title.

Warren Buffett. Considered by many to be the greatest investor in history, Warren Buffett hasn't written a book. He writes an annual letter to shareholders of Berkshire Hathaway, his hugely successful holding company. These missives, which are easy to find on the Internet, are eagerly awaited, and not just by his shareholders. Written with informal charm (a Google search for *warren buffett* together with *folksy* will yield thousands of results), they're often quotable. More importantly they offer a look at how an extraordinarily perceptive and disciplined investor approaches the subject.

The letters also display another of Buffett's unusual qualities: he has the moral strength to admit his mistakes, and not in the backhanded way we so often see from business and political leaders who accept responsibility but not blame. Buffett tells his shareholders in plain language what he did wrong and why it was wrong and how it cost them money. I can't help admiring that approach and thinking I should do the same if I ever make a mistake.

More than that, Buffett expresses a strong preference to do business with people of high integrity. If you want to work with him (as just about everyone in the world of business does) you need to show that you turn right corners. Buffett's emphasis on honesty hasn't hampered him at all; on the contrary, it's one of the keys to his success. That's a thought with which I'm pleased to end this book.

Acknowledgments

The sharp eye and thoughtful comments of my editor, Anna Mowry, greatly improved this book. The questionable judgment of my publisher in allowing me to change the text after her last review absolves her of any blame for errors.

The designer of this book's cover owes a debt of thanks for improvements suggested by Keith Philpott, and if the result is less elegant than a silk purse, surely it is because his starting point was a sow's ear.

I'm grateful to all the authors mentioned under *Further Reading* for the intellectual gift of understanding—and for the more pragmatic benefit of helping their readers, myself included, succeed as investors.

KAT

Index

Made in the USA
Lexington, KY
16 August 2010